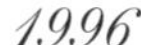

VOLUME III

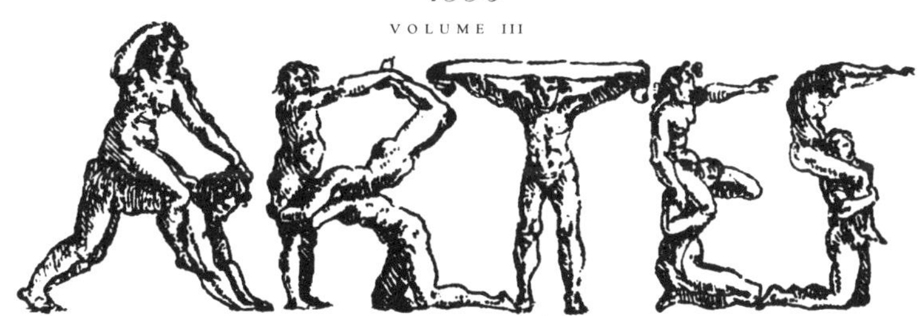

AN INTERNATIONAL READER OF LITERATURE ART AND MUSIC

Editors
Gunnar Harding and Bengt Jangfeldt

American editor Pat Strachan

In memory of Joseph Brodsky
1940–1996

Published by

MERCURY HOUSE
(USA)
and
NATUR OCH KULTUR
(SWEDEN)

ARTES
c/o Musikaliska Akademien
Blasieholmstorg 8. S-111 48 Stockholm
Tel. 46 8 611 50 48 Fax 46 8 611 87 18

American address:
329 East 10th Street. #10, New York, N.Y. 10009
Tel. 212 645-3346

Designed by Anders Ljungman and Johan Melbi

ARTES INTERNATIONAL
is published annually by Mercury House,
785 Market Street, Suite 1500, San Francisco, Ca. 94103
and distributed by Consortium Book Sales and Distribution,
1045 Westgate Drive, St. Paul, Mn. 55114

Although ARTES and ARTES INTERNATIONAL
are funded by the Swedish Academy,
the Academy of Fine Arts, the Academy of Music,
and the Society of Nine in Stockholm,
its editorial policy is entirely independent,
and the opinions expressed herein are solely
those of the editors and contributors

The editors wish to thank
Ann Kjellberg, Amy Robbins and Brina Gehry

Price per issue: $ 14.95
Two-year, postage-paid subscription: $ 25.00
(plus $ 5.00 postal surcharge for subscriptions
outside the U.S.). Please address subscription
and back-issue requests to
ARTES
329 East 10th Street. #10,
New York, N.Y. 10009

ISBN 1-56279-086-2

Printed by
Centraltryckeriet AB
Borås 1996

CONTENTS

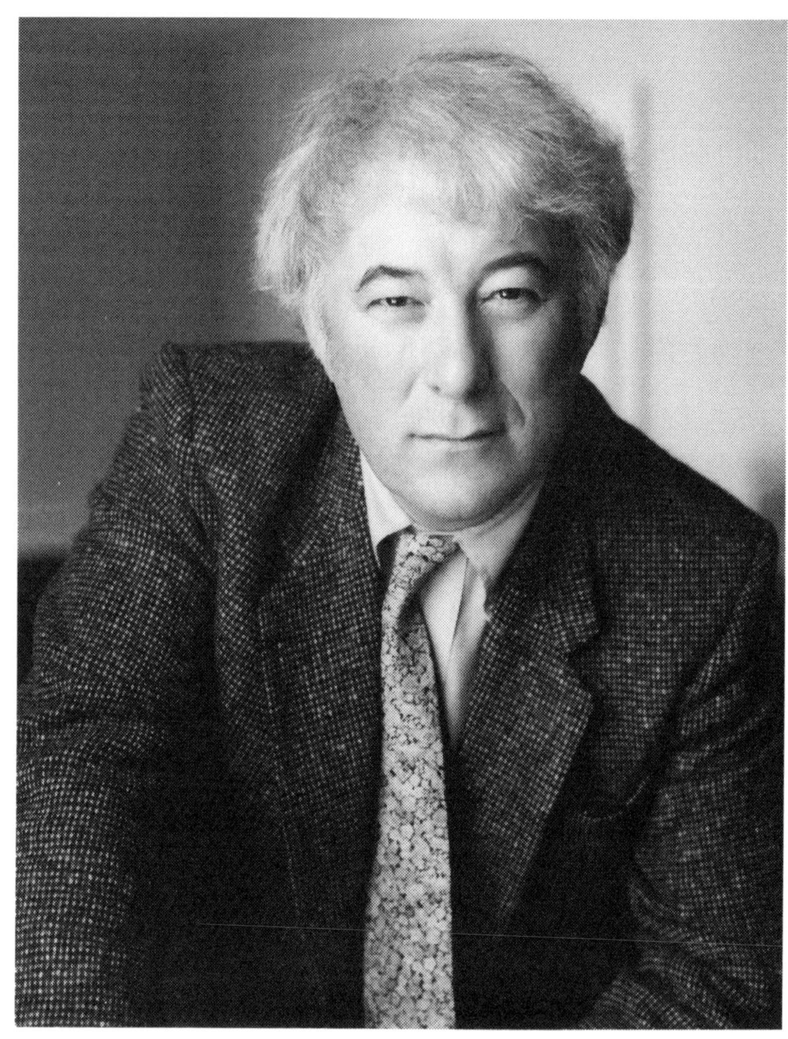

Seamus Heaney. Photo Jerry Bauer.

The Nobel Lecture

Crediting Poetry

SEAMUS HEANEY

When I first encountered the name of the city of Stockholm, I little thought that I would ever visit it, never mind end up being welcomed to it as a guest of the Swedish Academy and the Nobel Foundation. At that particular time, such an outcome was not just beyond expectation: it was simply beyond conception. In the 1940s, when I was the eldest child of an ever-growing family in rural Co. Derry, we crowded together in the three rooms of a traditional thatched farmstead and lived a kind of den-life which was more or less emotionally and intellectually proofed against the outside world. It was an intimate, physical, creaturely existence in which the night sounds of the horse in the stable beyond one bedroom wall mingled with the sounds of adult conversation from the kitchen beyond the other. We took in everything that was going on, of course — rain in the trees, mice on the ceiling, a steam train rumbling along the railway line one field back from the house — but we took it in as if we were in the doze of hibernation. Ahistorical, presexual, in suspension between the archaic and the modern, we were as susceptible and impressionable as the drinking water that stood in a bucket in our scullery: every time a passing train made the earth shake, the surface of that water used to ripple delicately, concentrically, and in utter silence.

But it was not only the earth that shook for us: the air around and above us was alive and signalling too. When a wind stirred in the beeches, it also stirred an aerial wire attached to the topmost branch of the chestnut tree. Down it swept, in through a hole bored in the corner of the kitchen window, right on into the innards of our wireless set, where a little pandemonium of burbles and squeaks would suddenly give way to the voice of a BBC newsreader speaking out of the unexpected like a *deus ex machina.* And that voice too we could hear in our bedroom, transmitting from beyond and behind the voices of the adults in the kitchen; just as we could often hear, behind and beyond every voice, the frantic, piercing signalling of Morse code.

We could pick up the names of neighbours being spoken in the local accents of our parents, and in the resonant English tones of the newsreader the names of bombers and of cities bombed, of war fronts and army divisions, the numbers of planes lost and of prisoners taken, of casualties suffered and advances made; and always, of course, we would pick up too those other, solemn and oddly bracing words, "the enemy" and "the allies." But even so, none of the news of these world-spasms entered me as terror. If there was something ominous in the newscaster's tones, there was something torpid about our understanding of what was at stake; and if there was something culpable about such political ignorance in that time and place, there was something positive about the security I inhabited as a result of it.

The wartime, in other words, was prereflective time for me. Preliterate too. Prehistorical in its way. Then as the years went on and my listening became more deliberate, I would climb up on an arm of our big sofa to get my ear closer to the wireless speaker. But it was still not the news that interested me; what I was after was the thrill of story, such as a detective serial about a British special agent called Dick Barton or perhaps a radio adaptation of one of Capt. W. E. Johns's adventure tales about an RAF flying ace called Biggles. Now that the other children were older and there was so much going on in the kitchen, I had to get close to the actual radio set in order to concentrate my hearing, and in that intent proximity to the dial I grew familiar with the names of foreign stations, with Leipzig and Oslo and Stuttgart and Warsaw and, of course, with Stockholm.

I also got used to hearing short bursts of foreign languages as the dial hand swept round from BBC to Radio Eireann, from the intonations of London to those of Dublin, and even though I did not understand what was being said in those first encounters with the gutturals and sibilants of European speech, I had already begun a journey into the wideness of the world beyond. This in turn became a journey into the wideness of language, a journey where each point of arrival — whether in one's poetry or one's life — turned out to be a stepping stone rather than a destination, and it is that journey which has brought me now to this honoured spot. And yet the platform here feels more like a space station than a stepping stone, so that is why, for once in my life, I am permitting myself the luxury of walking on air.

*

I credit poetry for making this space-walk possible. I credit it immediately because of a line I wrote fairly recently encouraging myself (and whoever else might be listening) to "walk on air against your better judgement." But I credit it ultimately because poetry can make an order as true to the impact of external reality and as sensitive to the inner laws of the poet's being as the ripples that rippled in and rippled out across the water in that scullery bucket fifty years ago. An order where we can at last grow up to that which we stored up as we grew. An order which satisfies all that is appetitive in the intelligence and prehensile in the affections. I credit poetry, in other words, both for being itself and for being a help, for making possible a fluid and restorative relationship between the mind's centre and its circumference, between the child gazing at the word "Stockholm" on the face of the radio dial and the man facing the faces that he meets in Stockholm at this most privileged moment. I credit it because credit is due to it, in our time and in all time, for its truth to life, in every sense of that phrase.

*

To begin with, I wanted that truth to life to possess a concrete reliability, and rejoiced most when the poem seemed most direct, an up-front representation of the world it stood in for or stood up for or stood its ground against. Even as a schoolboy, I loved John Keats's ode "To Autumn" for being an ark of the covenant between language and sensation; as an adolescent, I loved Gerard Manley Hopkins for the intensity of his exclamations, which were also equations for a rapture and an ache I didn't fully know I knew until I read him; I loved Robert Frost for his farmer's accuracy and his wily down-to-earthness; and Chaucer too for much the same reasons. Later on I would find a different kind of accuracy, a moral down-to-earthness to which I responded deeply and always will, in the war poetry of Wilfred Owen, a poetry where a New Testament sensibility suffers and absorbs the shock of the new century's barbarism. Then later again, in the pure consequence of Elizabeth Bishop's style, in the sheer obduracy of Robert Lowell's and in the barefaced confrontation of Patrick Kavanagh's, I encountered further reasons for believing in poetry's ability — and responsibility — to say what happens, to "pity the planet," to be "not concerned with Poetry."

This temperamental disposition towards an art that was earnest and devoted to things as they are was corroborated by the experience of having been born and brought up in Northern Ireland and of having lived with that place, even though I have lived out of it for the past quarter of a century. No place in the world prides itself more on its vigilance and realism, no place considers itself more qualified to censure any flourish of rhetoric or extravagance of aspiration. So, partly as a result of having internalized these attitudes through growing up with them, and partly as a result of growing a skin to protect myself against them, I went for years half-avoiding and half-resisting the opulence and extensiveness of poets as different as Wallace Stevens and Rainer Maria Rilke; crediting insufficiently the crystalline inwardness of Emily Dickinson, all those forked lightnings and fissures of association; and missing the visionary strangeness of Eliot. And these more or less costive attitudes were fortified by a refusal to grant the poet any more license than any other citizen; and they were further induced by having to conduct oneself as a poet in a situation of ongoing political violence and public expectation. A public expectation, it has to be said, not of poetry as such but of political positions variously approvable by mutually disapproving groups.

In such circumstances, the mind still longs to repose in what Samuel Johnson once called with superb confidence "the stability of truth," even as it recognizes the destabilizing nature of its own operations and enquiries. Without needing to be theoretically instructed, consciousness quickly realizes that it is the site of variously contending discourses. The child in the bedroom, listening simultaneously to the domestic idiom of his Irish home and the official idioms of the British broadcaster while picking up from behind both the signals of some other distress, that child was already being schooled for the complexities of his adult predicament, a future where he would have to adjudicate among promptings variously ethical, aesthetical, moral, political, metrical, sceptical, cultural, topical, typical, post-colonial and, taken all together, simply impossible. So it was that I found myself in the mid-1970s in another small house, this time in Co. Wicklow south of Dublin, with a young family of my own and a slightly less imposing radio set, listening to the rain in the trees and to the news of bombings closer to home — not only those by the Provisional IRA in Belfast but equally atrocious assaults in Dublin by loyalist paramilitaries from the north. Feeling puny in my predicaments as I read about the tragic logic of Osip Mandelstam's fate in the 1930s, feeling challenged yet steadfast in my noncombatant status when I heard, for example, that one particularly sweet-natured school friend had been interned without trial because he was suspected of having been involved in a political killing. What I was longing for was not quite stability but an active escape from the quicksand of relativism, a way of crediting poetry without anxiety or apology. In a poem called "Exposure," I wrote then:

> . . . If I could come on meteorite!
> Instead I walk through damp leaves,
> Husks, the spent flukes of autumn,

Imagining a hero
On some muddy compound,
His gift like a slingstone
Whirled for the desperate.

How did I end up like this?
I often think of my friends'
Beautiful prismatic counselling
And the anvil brains of some who hate me

As I sit weighing and weighing
My responsible *tristia.*
For what? For the ear? For the people?
For what is said behind-backs?

Rain comes down through the alders,
Its low conducive voices
Mutter about let-downs and erosions
And yet each drop recalls

The diamond absolutes.
I am neither internee nor informer;
An inner émigré, grown long-haired
And thoughtful; a wood-kerne

Escaped from the massacre,
Taking protective colouring
From bole and bark, feeling
Every wind that blows;

Who, blowing up these sparks
For their meagre heat, have missed
The once-in-a-lifetime portent,
The comet's pulsing rose.

(From *North,* 1975)

In one of the poems best known to students in my generation, a poem which could be said to have taken the nutrients of the symbolist movement and made them available in capsule form, the American poet Archibald MacLeish affirmed that "Poetry should be equal to/ not true." As a defiant statement of poetry's gift for telling truth but telling it slant, this is both cogent and corrective. Yet there are times when a deeper need enters, when we want the poem to be not only pleasurably right but compellingly wise, not only a surprising variation played upon the world, but a re-tuning of the world itself. We want the surprise to be transitive, like the impatient thump which unexpectedly restores the picture to the television set, or the electric shock which sets the fibrillating heart back to its proper rhythm. We want what the woman wanted in the prison queue in Leningrad, standing there blue with cold and whispering for fear, enduring the terror of Stalin's regime and asking the poet Anna Akhmatova if she could describe it all, if her art could be equal to it. And this is the want I too was experiencing in those far more protected circumstances in Co. Wicklow when I wrote the lines I have just quoted, a need for poetry that would merit the definition of it I gave a few moments ago, as an order "true to the impact of external reality and ... sensitive to the inner laws of the poet's being."

*

The external reality and inner dynamic of happenings in Northern Ireland between 1968 and 1974 were symptomatic of change — violent change admittedly, but change nevertheless, and for the minority living there, change had been long overdue. It should have come early, as the result of the ferment of protest on the streets in the late sixties, but that was not to be and the eggs of danger which were always incubating got hatched out very quickly. While the Christian moralist in oneself was impelled to deplore the atrocious nature of the IRA's campaign of bombings and killings, and the "mere Irish" in oneself was appalled by the ruthlessness of the British Army on occasions like Bloody Sunday in Derry in 1972, the minority citizen in oneself, the one who had grown up conscious that his group was distrusted and discriminated against in all kinds of official and unofficial ways, this citizen's perception was at one with the poetic truth of the situation in recognizing that if life in Northern Ireland were ever really to flourish, change had to take place. But that citizen's perception was also at one with the truth in recognizing that the very brutality of the means by which the IRA was pursuing change was destructive of the trust upon which new possibilities would have to be based.

Nevertheless, until the British government caved in to the strong-arm tactics of the Ulster loyalist workers after the Sunningdale Conference in 1974, a well-disposed mind could still hope to make sense of the circumstances, to balance what was promising with what was destructive and do what W. B. Yeats had tried to do half a century before, namely, "to hold in a single thought reality and justice." After 1974, however, for the twenty long years between then and the ceasefires of August 1994, such a hope proved impossible. The violence from below was then productive of nothing but a retaliatory violence from above, the dream of justice became subsumed into the callousness of reality, and people settled in to a quarter century of life-waste and spirit-waste, of hardening attitudes and narrowing possibilities that were the natural result of political solidarity, traumatic suffering and sheer emotional self-protectiveness.

*

One of the most harrowing moments in the whole history of the harrowing of the heart in Northern Ireland came when a minibus full of workers being driven home one January evening in 1976 was held up by armed and masked men and the occupants of the van ordered at gunpoint to line up at the side of the road. Then one of the masked executioners said to them, "Any Catholics among you, step out here." As it happened, this particular group, with one exception, were all Protestants, so the presumption must have been that the masked men were Protestant paramilitaries about to carry out a tit-for-tat sectarian killing of the Catholic as the odd man out, the one who would have been presumed to be in sympathy with the IRA and all its actions. It was a terrible moment for him, caught between dread and witness, but he did make a motion to step forward. Then, the story goes, in that split second of decision, and in the relative cover of the winter evening darkness, he felt the hand of the Protestant worker next to him take his hand and squeeze it in a signal that said no, don't move, we'll not betray you, nobody need know what faith or party you belong to. All in vain, however, for the man stepped out of the line; but instead of finding a gun at his temple, he was thrown backward and away as the gunmen opened fire on those remaining in the line, for these were not Protestant terrorists, but members, presumably, of the Provisional IRA.

*

It is difficult at times to repress the thought that history is about as instructive as an abattoir; that Tacitus was right and peace is merely the desolation left behind after the decisive operations of merciless power. I remember, for example, shocking myself with a thought I had about that friend who was imprisoned in the seventies upon suspicion of having been involved with a political murder: I shocked myself by thinking that even if he were guilty, he might still perhaps be helping the future to be born, breaking the repressive forms and liberating new potential in the only way that worked, that is to say the violent way — which therefore became, by extension, the right way. It was like a moment of exposure to interstellar cold, a reminder of the scary element, both inner and outer, in which human beings must envisage and conduct their lives. But it was only a moment. The birth of the future we desire is surely in the contraction which that terrified Catholic felt on the roadside when another hand gripped his hand, not in the gunfire that followed, so absolute and so desolate, if also so much a part of the music of what happens.

As writers and readers, as sinners and citizens, our realism and our aesthetic sense make us wary of crediting the positive note. The very gunfire braces us and the atrocious confers a worth upon the effort which it calls forth to confront it. We are rightly in awe of the torsions in the poetry of Paul Celan and rightly enamoured of the suspiring voice in Samuel Beckett, because these are evidence that art can rise to the occasion and somehow be the corollary of Celan's stricken destiny as Holocaust survivor and Beckett's demure heroism as a member of the French Resistance. Likewise, we are rightly suspicious of that which gives too much consolation in these circumstances; the very extremity of our late-twentieth-century knowledge puts much of our cultural heritage to an extreme test. Only the very stupid or the very deprived can any longer help knowing that the documents of civilization have been written in blood and tears, blood and tears no less real for being very remote. And when this intellectual predisposition coexists with the actualities of Ulster and Israel and Bosnia and Rwanda and a host of other wounded spots on the face of the earth, the inclination is not only not to credit human nature with much constructive potential but not to credit anything too positive in the work of art.

Which is why for years I was bowed to the desk like some monk bowed over his prie-dieu, some dutiful contemplative pivoting his understanding in an attempt to bear his portion of the weight of the world, knowing himself incapable of heroic virtue or redemptive effect, but constrained by his obedience to his rule to repeat the effort and the posture. Blowing up sparks for a meagre heat. Forgetting faith, straining towards good works. Attending insufficiently to the diamond absolutes, among which must be counted the sufficiency of that which is absolutely imagined. Then finally and happily, and not in obedience to the dolorous circumstances of my native place but in spite of them, I straightened up. I began a few years ago to try to make space in my reckoning and imagining for the marvellous as well as for the murderous. And once again I shall try to represent the import of that changed orientation with a story out of Ireland.

☆

This is a story about another monk holding himself up valiantly in the posture of endurance. It is said that once upon a time St. Kevin was kneeling with his arms stretched out in the form of a cross in Glendalough, a monastic site not too far from where we lived in Co. Wicklow, a place which to this day is one of the most wooded and watery retreats in the whole of the country. Anyhow, as Kevin knelt and prayed, a blackbird mistook his outstretched hand for some kind of roost and swooped down upon it, laid a clutch of eggs in it and proceeded to nest in it as if it were the branch of a tree. Then, overcome with pity and constrained by his faith to love the life in all creatures great and small, Kevin stayed immobile for hours and days and nights and weeks, holding out his hand until the eggs hatched and the fledglings grew wings, true to life if subversive of common sense, at the intersection of natural process and the glimpsed ideal, at one and the same time a signpost and a reminder. Manifesting that order of poetry where we can at last grow up to that which we stored up as we grew.

☆

St. Kevin's story is, as I say, a story out of Ireland. But it strikes me that it could equally well come out of India or Africa or the Arctic or the Americas. By which I do not mean merely to consign it to a typology of folktales, or to dispute its value by questioning its culture-bound status within a multicultural context. On the contrary, its trustworthiness and its travelworthiness have to do with its local setting. I can, of course, imagine it being deconstructed nowadays as a paradigm of colonialism, with Kevin figuring as the benign imperialist (or the missionary in the wake of the imperialist), the one who intervenes and appropriates the indigenous life and interferes with its pristine ecology. And I have to admit that there is indeed an irony that it was such a one who recorded and preserved this instance of the true beauty of the Irish heritage: Kevin's story, after all, appears in the writings of a Norman chronicler, Giraldus Cambrensis, one of the people who invaded Ireland in the twelfth century, one whom the Irish-language annalist Geoffrey Keating would call, five hundred years later, "the bull of the herd of those who wrote the false history of Ireland." But even so, I still cannot persuade myself that this manifestation of early

Christian civilization should be construed all that simply as a way into whatever is exploitative or barbaric in our history, past and present. The whole conception strikes me rather as being another example of the kind of work I saw a few weeks ago in the small museum in Sparta, on the morning before the news of this year's Nobel Prize in literature was announced.

This was art which sprang from a cult very different from the faith espoused by St. Kevin. Yet in it there was a representation of a roosted bird and an entranced beast and a self-enrapturing man, except that this time the man was Orpheus and the rapture came from music rather than prayer. The work itself was a small carved relief, and I could not help making a sketch of it; but neither could I help copying out the information typed on the card which accompanied and identified the exhibit. The image moved me because of its antiquity and durability, but the description on the card moved me also because it gave a name and credence to that which I see myself as having been engaged upon for the past three decades: "Votive panel," the identification card said, "possibly set up to Orpheus by local poet. Local work of the Hellenistic period."

*

Once again, I hope I am not being sentimental or simply fetishizing — as we have learnt to say — the local. I wish instead to suggest that images and stories of the kind I am invoking here do function as bearers of value. The century has witnessed the defeat of Nazism by force of arms; but the erosion of the Soviet regimes was caused by, among other things, the sheer persistence, beneath the imposed ideological conformity, of cultural values and psychic resistances of a kind that these stories and images enshrine. Even if we have learned to be rightly and deeply fearful of elevating the cultural forms and conservatisms of any nation into normative and exclusivist systems, even if we have terrible proof that pride in an ethnic and religious heritage can quickly degrade into the fascistic, our vigilance on that score should not displace our love and trust in the good of the indigenous per se. On the contrary, a trust in the staying power and travelworthiness of such good should encourage us to credit the possibility of a world where respect for the validity of every tradition will issue in the creation and maintenance of a salubrious political space. In spite of devastating and repeated acts of massacre, assassination and extirpation, the huge acts of faith which have marked the new relations between Palestinians and Israelis, Africans and Afrikaners, and the way in which walls have come down in Europe and iron curtains have opened, all this inspires a hope that new possibility can still open up in

Ireland as well. The crux of that problem involves an ongoing partition of the island between British and Irish jurisdictions, and an equally persistent partition of the affections in Northern Ireland between the British and Irish heritages; but surely every dweller in the country must hope that the governments involved in its governance can devise institutions which will allow that partition to become a bit more like the net on a tennis court, a demarcation allowing for agile give-and-take, for encounter and contending, prefiguring a future where the vitality that flowed in the beginning from those bracing words "enemy" and "allies" might finally derive from a less binary and altogether less binding vocabulary.

*

When the poet W. B. Yeats stood on this platform more than seventy years ago, Ireland was emerging from the throes of a traumatic civil war that had followed fast on the heels of a war of independence fought against the British. The struggle that ensued had been brief enough; it was over by May 1923, some seven months before Yeats sailed to Stockholm, but it was bloody, savage and intimate, and for generations to come it would dictate the terms of politics within the twenty-six independent counties of Ireland, that part of the island known first of all as the Irish Free State and then subsequently as the Republic of Ireland.

Yeats barely alluded to the civil war or the war of independence in his Nobel speech. Nobody understood better than he the connection between the construction or destruction of state institutions and the founding or foundering of cultural life, but on this occasion he chose to talk instead about the Irish Dramatic Movement. His story was about the creative purpose of that movement, and its historic good fortune in having not only his own genius to sponsor it, but also the genius of his friends John Millington Synge and Lady Augusta Gregory. He came to Sweden to tell the world that the local work of poets and dramatists had been as important to the transformation of his native place and times as the ambushes of guerrilla armies. His boast in that elevated prose was essentially the same as the one he would make in verse more than a decade later in his poem "The Municipal Gallery Revisited." There Yeats presents himself among the portraits and heroic narrative paintings which celebrate the events and personalities of recent history, and all of a sudden he realizes that something truly epoch-making has occurred: "'This is not,' I say, / 'The dead Ireland of my youth, but an Ireland / The poets have imagined, terrible and gay.'" And the poem concludes with two of the most quoted lines of his entire œuvre:

Think where man's glory most begins and ends,
And say my glory was I had such friends.

And yet, expansive and thrilling as these lines are, they are an instance of poetry flourishing itself rather than proving itself, they are the poet's lap of honour, and in this respect if in no other they resemble what I am doing in this lecture. In fact, I should quote here on my own behalf some other words from the poem: "You that would judge me, do not judge alone/This book or that." Instead, I ask you to do what Yeats asked his audience to do and think of the achievement of Irish poets and dramatists and novelists over the past forty years, among whom I am proud to count great friends. In literary matters, Ezra Pound advised against accepting the opinion of those "who haven't themselves produced notable work," and it is advice I have been privileged to follow, since it is the good opinion of notable workers — and not just those in my own country — that has fortified my endeavour since I began to write in Belfast more than thirty years ago.

Yeats, however, was by no means all flourish. To the credit of poetry in our century there must surely be entered in any reckoning his two great sequences of poems entitled "Nineteen Hundred and Nineteen" and "Meditations in Time of Civil War," the latter of which contains the famous lyric about the bird's nest at his window, where a starling or stare had built in a crevice of the old wall. The poet was living then in a Norman tower which had been very much a part of the military history of the country in earlier and equally troubled times, and as his thoughts turned upon the irony of civilizations being consolidated by violent and powerful conquerors who end up commissioning the artists and the architects, he began to associate the sight of a mother bird feeding its young with the image of the honey-bee, an image deeply lodged in poetic tradition and always suggestive of the ideal of an industrious, harmonious, nurturing commonwealth:

The bees build in the crevices
Of loosening masonry, and there
The mother birds bring grubs and flies.
My wall is loosening; honey-bees,
Come build in the empty house of the stare.

We are closed in, and the key is turned
On our uncertainty; somewhere
A man is killed, or a house burned,
Yet no clear fact to be discerned:
Come build in the empty house of the stare.

A barricade of stone or of wood;
Some fourteen days of civil war;
Last night they trundled down the road
That dead young soldier in his blood:
Come build in the empty house of the stare.

We had fed the heart on fantasies,
The heart's grown brutal from the fare;
More substance in our enmities
Than in our love; O honey-bees,
Come build in the empty house of the stare.

I have heard this poem repeated often, in whole and in part, by people in Ireland over the past twenty-five years, and no wonder, for it is as tender-minded towards life itself as St. Kevin was and as tough-minded about what happens in and to life as Homer. It knows that the massacre will happen again on the roadside, that the workers in the minibus are going to be lined up and shot down just after quitting time; but it also credits as a reality the squeeze of the hand, the actuality of sympathy and protectiveness between living creatures. It satisfies the contradictory needs which consciousness experiences at times of extreme crisis, the need on the one hand for a truth-telling that will be hard and retributive, and on the other hand, the need not to harden the mind to a point where it denies its own yearnings for sweetness and trust. It is a proof that poetry can be equal to *and* true at the same time, an example of that completely adequate poetry which the Russian woman sought from Anna Akhmatova, and which William Wordsworth produced at a corresponding moment of historical crisis and personal dismay almost exactly two hundred years ago.

*

When the bard Demodocus sings of the fall of Troy and of the slaughter that accompanied it, Odysseus weeps and Homer says that his tears were like the tears of a wife on a battlefield weeping for the death of a fallen husband. His epic simile continues in Robert Fitzgerald's translation:

> At the sight of the man panting and dying there,
> she slips down to enfold him, crying out;
> then feels the spears, prodding her back and shoulders,
> and goes bound into slavery and grief.
> Piteous weeping wears away her cheeks:
> but no more piteous than Odysseus' tears,
> cloaked as they were, now, from the company.

Even today, three thousand years later, as we channel-surf over so much live coverage of contemporary savagery, highly informed but nevertheless in danger of growing immune, familiar to the point of overfamiliarity with old newsreels of the concentration camp and the gulag, Homer's image can still bring us to our senses. The callousness of those spear shafts on the woman's back and shoulders survives time and translation. The image has that documentary adequacy which answers all that we know about the intolerable.

But there is another kind of adequacy which is specific to lyric poetry. This has to do with the "temple inside our hearing" which the passage of the poem calls into being. It is an adequacy deriving from what Mandelstam called "the steadfastness of speech articulation," from the resolution and independence which the entirely realized poem sponsors. It has as much to do with the energy released by linguistic fission and fusion, with the buoyancy generated by cadence and tone and rhyme and stanza, as it has to do with the poem's concerns or the poet's truthfulness. In fact, in lyric poetry, truthfulness becomes recognizable as a ring of truth within the medium itself. And it is the unappeasable pursuit of this note, a note tuned to its most extreme in Emily Dickinson and Paul Celan and orchestrated to its most opulent in John Keats, it is this which keeps the poet's ear straining to hear the totally persuasive voice behind all the other informing voices.

Which is a way of saying that I have never quite climbed down from the arm of that sofa. I may have grown more attentive to the news and more alive to the world history and world-sorrow behind it. But the thing uttered by the speaker I strain towards is still not quite the story of what is going on. It is more reflexive than that, because as a poet I am straining towards a strain, in the sense that the effort is to repose in the stability conferred by a musically satisfying order of sounds. As if the ripple at its widest desired to be verified by a reformation of itself, to be drawn in and drawn out through its point of origin.

I also strain towards this in the poetry I read. And I find it, for example, in the repetition of that refrain of Yeats's, "Come build in the empty house of the stare," with its tone of supplication, its pivots of strength in the words "build" and "house" and its acknowledgement of dissolution in the word "empty." I find it also in the triangle of forces held in equilibrium by the triple rhyme of "fantasies" and "enmities" and "honey-bees," and in the sheer in-placeness of the whole poem as a given form within the language. Poetic form is both the ship and the anchor. It is at once a buoyancy and a steadying, allowing for the simultaneous gratification of whatever is centrifugal and whatever is centripetal in mind and body. And it is by such means that Yeats's work does what the necessary poetry always does, which is to touch the base of our sympathetic nature while taking in at the same time the unsympathetic nature of the world to which that nature is constantly exposed. The form of the poem, in other words, is crucial to poetry's power to do the thing which always is and always will be to poetry's credit: the power to persuade that vulnerable part of our consciousness of its rightness in spite of the evidence of wrongness all around it; the power to remind us that we are hunters and gatherers of values, that our very solitudes and distresses are creditable, insofar as they, too, are an earnest of our veritable human being.

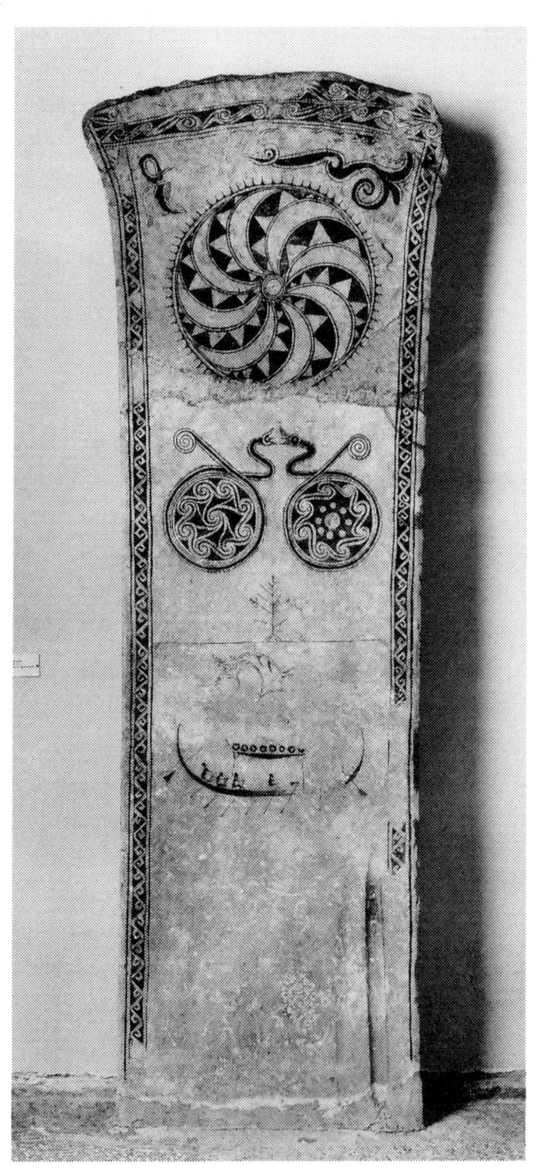

Picture stone, Sanda, Gotland, ca. A.D. 400–500.
Photo Raymond Hejdström. © Gotlands Fornsal.

THE SEAFARER

"The Seafarer" is the nineteenth-century name for an untitled, anonymous Anglo-Saxon poem. Its unique manuscript, inscribed in about A.D. 975, has been preserved at Exeter Cathedral, England, since A.D. 1072. The poem's content, although in many ways typical of its age, is nevertheless timeless, commonplace, and ancient. The image of life as a voyage and death as a sea-passage to an unknown country can be traced to prehistoric Sumeria and Egypt, where the concept of the Boat of the Dead originated in the fourth millennium B.C. Forms of ship-burial were continuous in Northern Europe from about 1500 B.C. to A.D. 900 or later. Many churches in Sweden and elsewhere are still furnished with models of ships suspended above the nave, a word which means "ship."

This is the truth of how I toiled
distraught, for days on end,
enduring care and bitter bile
within my breast, my keel cleaving
endless halls of heaving waves.

I would often at the bark's bows wake
the strait night through, steering
her clear of clashing cliffs.

Cold fetters froze my feet
and hunger seared my heart
with sore sea-weariness.

That man lolling on fair land
has no earthly inkling of how I,
a wretched wreck in ice-cold seas,
weathered each winter
exiled from kith and kin.

Hail scoured my skin, and hoar
hung heavy.

All I ever heard along the ice-way
was sounding sea; the gannet's shanty,
whooper and curlew calls and mewling gull
were all my gaming, mead and mirth.
At tempest-tested granite crags
the ice-winged tern would taunt;
spray-feathered ospreys overhead
would soar and scream.

No kinsman near to fend off need,
no one to comfort or console.

That fine fellow, carefree in his cups,
set snugly up in town, cannot conceive
the load I hauled along the sea-lanes.

Night shadows deepen; northern snow
hardens the soil and hail hits earth
like cold corn.

Yet my heart hammers now, yearning anew,
wanting the steep salt-water road,
longing with lust to roam rough seas, alone
to seek out some far foreign shore:
the mood to wander mills within my mind.

But none on earth may be so proud
so prodigal or yare in youth,
nor so express in action,
nor favoured by so mild a master
that he embark without dark doubt;
what end for him the Master may intend.

He will not heed the harp though
and is not gladdened by gold rings
nor woman's winning ways

and wants no worldly joys;
only the rolling oceans urge him on,
the wave play pulls him and impels.

Then blossom decks the bower's bough
and flowers fill the meads;
the bothie blooms: all life
begins to lift; its fever floods
his feelings and the full tides tug
upon him from afar.

What's more, the gowk with plaintive geck
is heralding his summer hoard of pain,
foreboding bitterness of breast.

Soft-bedded bloods cannot conceive
what some men suffer as abroad
they travel tracks of exile.

Reckless of that, my thought is thrown
beyond my heart's cage now. Hot hunger
keenly comes again; my mind is cast
upon the sea-swell, over the whale's world,
widely to course creation's coast.

The lone call wails above on wing:
it steels the unarmed soul to start
across the waters where the whale sways.

God's visions are to me more vivid
than fleeting life on dry dead land;
and earthly wealth will not endure.

Still three things twist man's mind
until the day his doom is sealed:

age, illness or some stroke of hate
will seize sense from him.

So any noble spirit will aspire to earn
an everlasting epitaph of praise
for good deeds done on earth: bold blows
dealt at the Devil and against fell foes
before he passes, that posterity
delights enjoyed for ever by the brave
among the angels may perpetuate.

The days of glory have decayed,
the earth has spilled its splendour;
there are no captains now, no kings,
gold-givers such as once there were,
the lords who lived with far-flung fame,
great men of glorious and good renown.

Virtue is fallen, visions are faded;
the weak are left to hold this world
worn low. The flower of the field is old,
the leaf is withered, and the laurel sere.
Throughout this middle isthmus man
meets age hoar-headed, bleak of face,
by former friends forsaken, groaning for
scions of lineage long since gone.

Life ebbs; the flesh feels less,
and fails to savour sweet or sour,
is frail of hand, feeble of mind.
Though men may bury treasured pelf
beside their brother's born remains
and sow his grave with golden goods,
he goes where gold is worthless.

Translated by Charles Harrison Wallace

CHARLES HARRISON WALLACE grew up in Scotland, Sweden, and England, and graduated in English Literature from Brasenose College, Oxford. He has translated three books from Swedish into English and published essays on a variety of subjects, including two monographs on the eighteenth-century English marine painter Peter Monamy. He is an experienced yacht crewman in Arctic waters. Since 1986, he has been a lecturer at the London Institute.

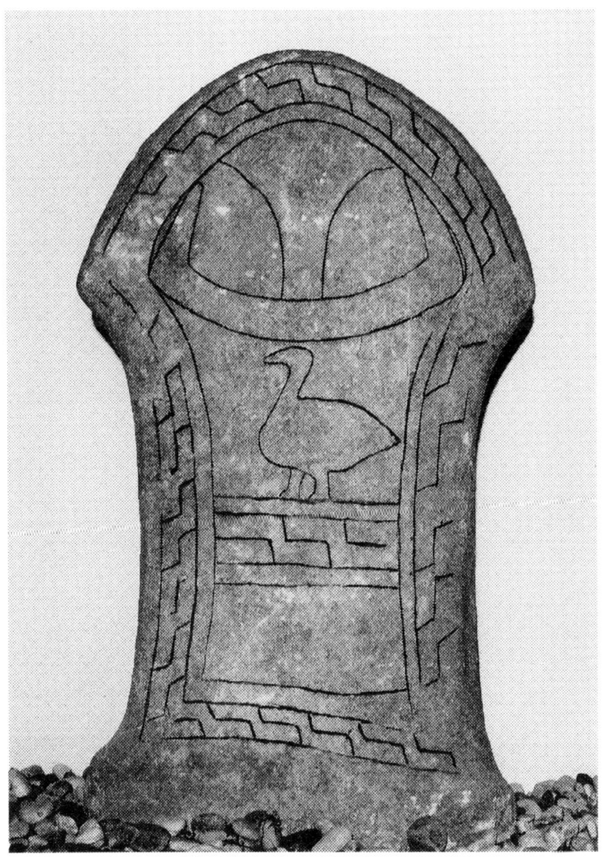

Picture stone, Smiss, Gotland, ca. A.D. 500–700. Photo Waldemar Falck.
© Gotlands Fornsal.

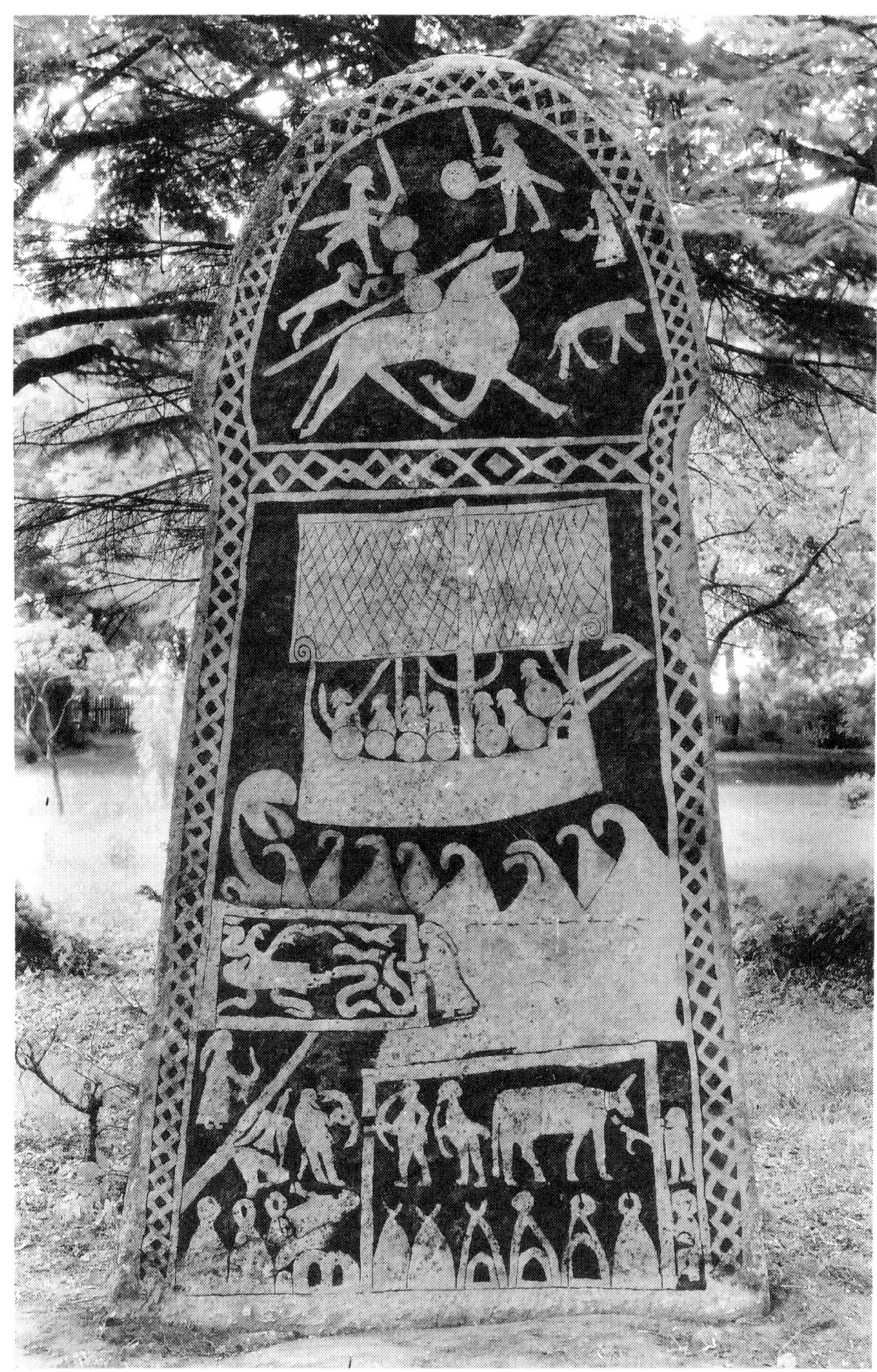

Picture stone, Hunninge parish, Gotland. Photo H. Faith-Ell.

A Trip to Gotland

ULF LINDE

The will to image:
— Morality detaches itself from convention and works toward only one end: to hone the sense of measure and weight.

That sentence, a quote, popped into my mind not too long ago, as I was looking at one of the picture stones in the island of Gotland's Hall of Antiquities. It is a three-meter-tall hunk of limestone, its surface ground flat, on which someone, long ago, glorified the deeds and dreams of his time in shallow relief carving.

When no one was looking, I stroked the stone. Even though it felt rough against my fingertips, it also felt inconceivably distant. Between the stone and my skin lay a millennium — alien time, not mine.

Then a fly, presumably the last one in Visby for the season, landed on the masterpiece. Cold and sluggish, it crawled across one glorious shape after another; it existed entirely in its own soon-to-be-ended time. The millennium did not bother it. It bothered only my somewhat literate species.

I had learned that this stone had been erected at Hunninge, in Gottard's Klinte parish, around A.D. 1,000 and that it, like other, similar stones, had stood by the side of a highway. It had been put there to be seen by many. I knew that the wealthy voyagers of the island had traveled in ships like the one carved by the unknown artist, and that they had traveled far and wide; this, presumably, was the reason why the carving showed both Irish and Carolingian, and perhaps even Byzantine, stylistic traits.

A figure surrounded by plaited-work was assumed to be Gunnar in the Snake Yard, a motif from the Lay of Sigurd in the Edda; if this was indeed the case, the plaited-work represented snakes, and a fuzzy, eroded shape next to the figure was probably a harp — the hero's instrument.

"Probably…" What was known was deplorably inadequate for an attempt to bridge the gap in time. Most of it was conjecture. It wasn't even possible to state with any certainty why these huge gateways to Elsewhere had been erected. They could not be opened.

Nevertheless, the forms were plain to see. Anyone could tell that the carvers of these stones were beholden to strict conventions, to stereotypes. Thus, all the human figures were rendered in profile. But why? The borrowings from the Irish were obvious; but in Ireland, faces were presented frontally. This was never the case here on Gotland. Whence such a prejudice?

While I was groping around in this practically empty past, the fly continued its walk across the stone. Watching it, I had an absurd intuition. They say that history illuminates the past; but does it really? It was the historical perspective that had opened up a chasm of extinguished time. The demiurge of history must have uttered the most insolent of all creation words: Let it be dark! And it became dark. At least for someone like me. Not for the fly — but then, it had never listened to words at all.

A pale, rough limestone surface, transformed by history into an abstract space, extinguished, except for a few fixed stars called facts, and a swarm of meteors called hypotheses: not enough light to steer by.

Little by little, unaware of it at first, I extricated myself from that space. I began to see the figures one by one, to understand what differentiated them, without — as previously — looking for the characteristics they shared, the style, the enigmatic conventions of ancient Gotland. Suddenly, I saw the seven men aboard the ship: the first one, in the stem, harsh and confident, the second calm and resolute, the third lively and curious (he seemed to be following a bird with his gaze), the fourth as principled as the fifth was unreliable, the sixth greedy and short-tempered, and the seventh, the helmsman, typically prudent and strong. I recognized them; they are present here, in this room — only their sartorial styles have changed.

Before long, I began to see the carved waves in a similar fashion. What I had perceived as a stereotype — an upside-down fishhook, repeated over and over — became choppy seas, the likes of which I had seen in Visby harbor that very morning. On another stone, the waves were drawn as a series of triangles with braid ornaments at their apices: these were foam-topped waves, driven by a serious gale. Then I went on to recognize one such detail after another.

Neither those clever clichés, nor the concepts they represent, nor the way in which proportions shift with each repeated form, each stereotype, are what makes these carvings so marvelous. That quality comes from what shines through these adjustments: a reality perceived by the senses — all five of them: the snake yard reeks, the venom stings, the waves hiss. What is marvelous about these shapes is their poetry.

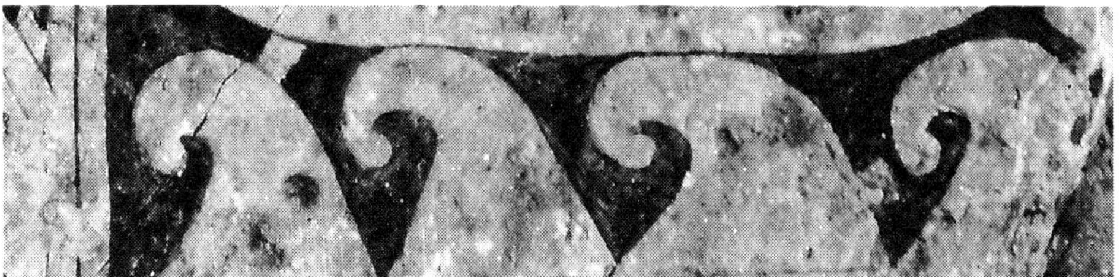

Picture stone, Hejnum parish, Gotland. Detail.

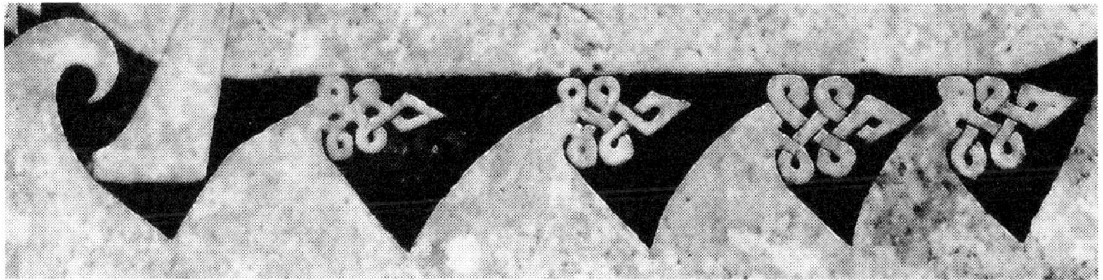

Picture stone, Hejnum parish, Gotland. Detail. Photo H. Faith-Ell.

It has been said that people of the Viking era took little interest in the individuality of creatures and things. But if that was the case, why did the Prophetess of the Voluspa not simply state that Modsogner and Durin manufactured a certain number of human figures out of clay? Why, instead, did she choose to enumerate the dwarf creations, one by one:

Nye and Nide
Nordre and Sudre
Austre and Västre
Alltjov, Dvalin
Bivor, Bavor
Bombur, Nore
An and Anar
Ae, Mjodvitner

And that is just the first stanza: the list of names goes on for four more, which isn't exactly indicative of an undeveloped sense of individuality. Why should the thought-patterns of the picture-stone carvers have been any different? Their adherence to convention did not prevent them from expressing, by means of slight shifts of proportion, what lies beyond convention: the uniqueness of creatures and things, the simple fact that Nye was not Nide, even though both of them were dwarves.

Thus, it was not so strange at all that my epigraph popped into my mind as I stood looking at the stone from Hunninge:

> *The will to image:*
> *— Morality detaches itself from convention and works toward only one end: to hone the sense of measure and weight.*

*

For a while, I was unable to place that quote. Its source lay in a context far removed from that stone. Then I remembered. It came from a book by Hugo Ball, the German poet, intellectual, anarchist, pacifist, who spent World War I in exile in Switzerland. In 1916, he and a few associates started a cabaret in a tavern on Zurich's Spiegelgasse, the Cabaret Voltaire. The group's deceptively infantile code word, Dada, went on to make history.

The Hunninge stone had evoked a Dadaist quote. Life is full of surprises.

Back on the mainland, I located the source. The quote came from *Die Flucht aus der Zeit (The Flight Out of Time)*, Ball's posthumously published journals, and was dated March 30, 1917. The shadow of an index finger seemed to sweep across the page — and I knew whose it was…

In the spring of 1962, I took the participants in a package tour arranged by the Friends of Stockholm's Museum of Modern Art to see the tavern on Spiegelgasse — it was, indeed, still there. According to our tour program, I was to give a lecture on Dada when we arrived in Zurich, and it seemed appropriate to deliver it in Cabaret Voltaire's old home. I was more than a little nervous, since one of our number was a person who, I gathered, did not suffer extravagant statements gladly: my predecessor on this [Swedish Academy] seat, Eyvind Johnson. When, in my lecture, I got to Hugo Ball, an esoteric writer, I took particular care to limit myself to a few quotes I had found in a Dada anthology. These, however, aroused Eyvind Johnson's interest, and after the lecture he asked me where he could find more of Ball's writing.

I told him I wasn't sure; the quotes in the anthology were all I knew — Ball's works were long out of print and impossible to find.

A few days later, Johnson made me a present of a copy of *Die Flucht aus der Zeit* he had found in an antiquarian book shop. "A lovely title," he said and handed it to me, opened to the entry dated March 30, 1917. He read it out loud, following the lines with his index finger, and said: "I wouldn't be ashamed to have written something like that myself."

He had written something like that himself — this, for instance, in the voice of Krilon:

> If a man who tries to re-experience such things in his soul is able to tear a single living image out of the solid block of suffering of this murderous reality — then all of that reality appears in front of his eyes ... To others, who have stopped at the bloodstained horror of statistics, unable to comprehend, to believe that such things happened only a hundred leagues from Sweden, that mediating act of fiction may let them know what it was really like.

Few have been as preoccupied by the difference between fiction and history as Eyvind Johnson, who insisted that a writer does not do what the historian does; he looks for very different kinds of truth. While the historian comes up with facts and the connections that existed between them, the writer's task is the one Johannes Lupigis performs in *Hans nådes tid (His Lordship's Time)*:

> He called forth the image, caught it out of the darkness, time and again. That was all he did, that was the great task he performed; such was his work, his preoccupation with time in the timeless.

As the quote indicates, Eyvind Johnson tended to put an equalsign between fiction and image. A poem or tale had to be graphic, something to be seen — even if only with an inner eye. This agrees with what Örjan Lindberger tells us in his biography of Johnson: All three portraits of women in *Några steg mot tystnaden (A Few Steps Toward Silence)* were based on the same Holbein drawing. That was what they looked like. Eyvind Johnson called for the precise image when he wrote:

> I look for details ... I look for faces, somewhere.

When he encountered such a face — perhaps one long dead, one seen by Holbein — it was not enough for him to approach it in the past. He felt compelled to meet its gaze in the present. He also wrote:

> To penetrate the past so that you are there — and, lo and behold, I am there now, and I say: The remembrance is here, and it belongs to what is alive, it belongs to life in the present.

The locus of his own present was where he waited for the face — or rather: the image of that face — to appear. Just as the environment can only show itself to the eye in the present, since the retina knows no other time, and just as the objects of the environment, at that moment, exist immutably exactly where they do exist — here! nowhere else — so a trace of the past may in remembrance arise before the inner eye, as a kind of transparent distillate, in the present, as an object equal in presence to the external ones, equally independent of the beholder, equally individuated: what once was, now is exactly what is seen, and nothing else. For Eyvind Johnson, an image must have been one of those transparent objects.

If so, it was an image of precisely that kind that appeared to me on the Hunninge stone. *Nota bene,* I am not referring to the agglomerate of stereotypical figures someone carved a thousand years ago. That image no longer belongs to life. Only after I saw the figures one by one, after I became aware of what differentiated them — I am tempted to say, when I had honed my sense of measure, of weight — the stone came to life in the present.

Within the stone was another, timeless image, one not made out of stone.

☆

The sense of measure and weight to which these stones testify was kept alive on Gotland long into the Christian era. An overwhelming testimonial to that fact is the north portal of Hablingbo church, carved around 1160 by the anonymous mason who Johnny Roosval called Magister Majestatis. His skill in getting even the roughest simplifications to express the fragility of all that lives, in glances and gestures, reminds one of Goya's: the image within the image keeps detaching itself from the carved stone and becomes poetry.

By the middle of the fifteenth century, the tradition was lost. Times were hard, once-wealthy Gotland impoverished. The only prosperous enterprise, it seems, was a workshop that provided the island churches with lime-wash frescoes. The master and his apprentices were active for several decades and managed to paint at least two churches every summer. Understandably, they wasted no time on subtleties. Wherever they went, they presented the scenes of Christ's passion in the same uniform way, clearly working from prepared stencils attached to the north wall of the nave — always only there — and filling in the outlines with paint. The only problem they had to deal with was the forced omission of one scene or another wherever the wall wasn't wide enough. This busy entrepreneur's name is unknown, but in the literature he is referred to as the Passion Master. Some have granted his work a

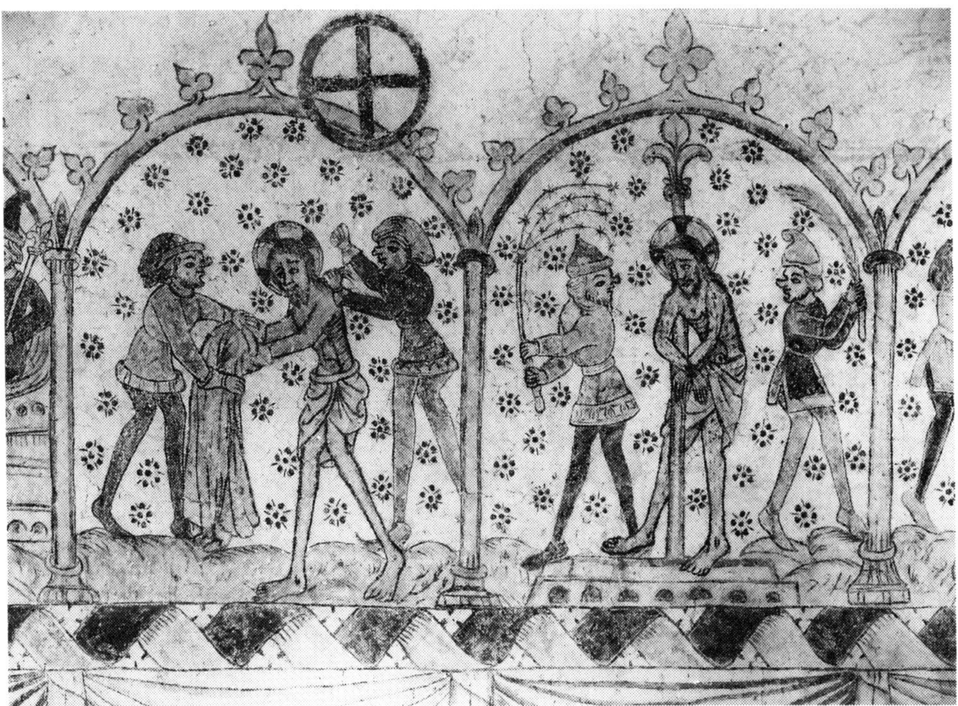

From the Passion suite in Sanda church, Gotland.

measure of pious naïveté, but their opinion must be based on a misinterpretation of faded spots: the paintings are truly execrable.

In the Passion Master's day, Christ's suffering was a heavily exploited motif. The mendicant friars, the period's arbiters of piety, liked to use it in their sermons in order to convince the members of their audiences that they weren't much better than Christ's torturers. As soon as they had realized this, and were all choked up with their sinfulness, they were ready for the pardoners' wares.

Looking at the tricks employed by the Passion Master, one may well imagine the blatancy of those sermons. The cumulative effect of these feasts of pain and baseness is one of the merely grotesque — as, for instance, when the "master" not only places Jews' hats on the two henchmen who are depicted whipping Christ, but also distorts their noses in the most extraordinary fashion. He may have heard that Jews were supposed to have hooked noses; he cannot have seen any such thing — if he had, he wouldn't have made the obscene appendages point up instead of down.

In the Passion Master, the will to image has withered. Even though he paints a nose, a mouth, two eyes, no face arises out of his scratchings. He has never managed to "tear a single living image out of the solid block of suffering of this murderous reality," as Eyvind Johnson put it. Hence, the raw paint has never achieved a present, a now.

Confronted with these meaningless simulacra of human expression — at Rone, Sanda, Endre, wherever — one only has to reverse Hugo Ball's aphorism to explain their wretchedness:

> Without the will to image, morality detaches itself from
> the sense of measure and weight and becomes mere convention.

*

Having reached this point in my essay, I wondered if I hadn't missed something. After all, the peasants who paid for the Passion Master's products must have appreciated what he gave them for their money. What, then, was it they saw?

Reading a recent article by Rudolf Zeitler, I approached an answer to that question. Zeitler summarizes his view of the paintings as follows: "Whether the phenomenon is a matter for art historians to consider is an open question; it may well be a subject for anthropologists to investigate."

I had missed the fact that these paintings had nothing whatsoever to do with art, that they never had had anything to do with art. To rephrase that: I had assumed that they were intended to express human experience, while their purpose clearly had been altogether different. The Passion Master had worked for a pious ideal. He had dedicated himself to what today is called "influencing public opinion" — an activity that pays no attention to the fact that every human being is unique.

We see it every day: the unique human being is punched in the nose he or she must have in order to ensure that every viewer "gets" the message. Today's Passion Masters are just as deficient in their sense of weight and measure.

"A Trip to Gotland" was presented at the Swedish Academy's ceremonial meeting on December 20, 1990.

Translated from the Swedish by Anselm Hollo

ULF LINDE is an art historian and art critic, and member of The Swedish Academy. He has written several books about Swedish artists and is director of the Thielska Galleriet in Stockholm. ANSELM HOLLO was born in Finland and has lived in the United States since 1967. He is a poet and translator from Swedish, Finnish, German, and French. He teaches at the Naropa Institute in Colorado.

How Tedious It Is to Be a Bureaucrat

A Biographical Collage of Anders Sparrman: Traveller, Botanist, and Practitioner of Magnetism in the Last Days of the Enlightenment

OTTO FAGERSTEDT AND SVERKER SÖRLIN

At first he was a traveller. His doctoral dissertation was entitled "Iter in Chinam" (*Travels in China*); he was a mere twenty years of age when he defended it for Linnæus in Uppsala. By that time he had already visited the Far East once. And he sailed constantly, until he reached the age of forty and suddenly stopped, moving in increasingly limited circles. From having appeared in the evening dress of the Enlightenment, as the years passed he clad himself in the motley of the self-appointed outsider and mystic.

But all this actually fits together in the best of all possible worlds. A man who dedicated his life to the natural sciences. A man rich in talent, with some degree of success, who remained a pauper. A lonely man. A capable man, but a bohemian who had difficulties fulfilling the duties of the bureaucrat.

The man we meet in the international encyclopædia as the cataloguer of the Cape's flora and James Cook's companion in the southern Polar Sea — who was he? The material available is limited: roughly one hundred letters, a number of scholarly publications, a few decidedly less scholarly. Some contemporary evaluations, none of them particularly wellfounded. If the truth about an individual exists, then it exists only as long as he himself does. Posterity dedicates itself to various attempts at clarification. But perhaps one can see this in another light. What if there is no truth in history, beyond the trivial fact that that which has happened has indeed happened?

A seventeen-year-old who travels to China needs to be independent. If he is not beforehand, then he becomes so during the course of the trip. He also learns how to see. He who travels as a mature adult risks remaining blind to everything new; for him, there is nothing new under the sun. Anders Sparrman left no diary of his trip to China, so we do not know what happened to him there. And he would continue to remain silent for a few more years. He turns up in the archives for the first time as the correspondent of Linnæus. He writes to report on a trip to the Cape Colony in South Africa. He speaks of his discoveries. It seems that being forced to submit a report opens the literary floodgates. The South African journey was arranged with the partial assistance of his teacher, Linnæus.

> We have now been given the opportunity to send a Swedish student, who moreover possesses insight into the natural sciences, to spend two to four years in the Cape Colony, including room and board. The East India Company in Gothenburg

> have in answer to my persistent pleas agreed to provide him with free passage on its ship Stockholms slott ... To undertake this journey I have appointed Studiosum Sparrman Uplandum who exhibits spirit, insight into these things and desire, but who is otherwise indigent. The price of a trip from here to Gothenburg is dear; to come to a foreign place without a farthing in one's purse is hazardous.
>
> Linnæus to the Academy of Sciences, recorded in the minutes of the Academy, November 13, 1771.

AT THE CAPE

It appears as though the patriarch of Uppsala did not have quite as good a hand with Sparrman as with the travelling apostles he sent out into the world in previous decades. Sparrman goes his own way. We know quite a lot about what Sparrman did in the Cape, where he arrived on the East India Company's ship in April 1772. We know because he sent letters from there, but mainly we know because he edited and published his diary in book form as *Resa till Goda hopps-udden, södra polkretsen och omkring jordklotet* (*A Voyage to the Cape of Good Hope, toward the Antarctic Polar Circle and around the World*), whose first volume appeared in 1783, the other two following much later. Swiftness in the dispensing of his duties does not seem to have been one of Anders Sparrman's foremost assets. The first part of the diary was written by Sparrman when he was between thirty and thirty-five years of age. He was neither very young nor particularly old. The twinkle is still there in his eye, he enjoys a little levity, and yet still makes claims to strict scholarship in his text. He does not wish to utter a syllable about anything that he does not know for certain. He seems every inch the empiricist, the accurate observer.

> Of those who have been tempted by curiosity to leave their Fatherlands, in order to chase their fate around the World, even through the land of the Hottentotts and Wildernesses, I have been led to understand that stories of very amusing and wonderful subjects are expected. One has good reason to expect such stories. Everywhere I went I met Nature in its manifoldness, always marvellous, oftimes delightful, occasionally terrifying. However, many of the rarities, of which one has read in the writings of others and about which I have been asked, must be absent in my Diary. One-footed Men, Cyclopses, Sirens, Nightmen ... and similar creatures of the imagination must needs disappear from the surface of our enlightened World; however many have up to now been led to believe no less remarkable fairy tales, with which Authors, who have visited and described the Hottentotts before me, have seasoned their stories, in order to make them attractive. Thus it ought not come as a surprise if the reader finds my stories to be very different from those of my numerous predecessors...
>
> *Resa till Goda hopps-udden, södra polkretsen och omkring jordklotet*, 1:4–5.

In other words, Anders Sparrman is a man of science. He describes the gathering of plants and he notes ethnographic details. He possesses a clarity of style which provides an open account, refusing to hide anything. But now and again he seems to forget his scientific ambitions. Suddenly he begins to tell a story.

> I rode up to a Farmhouse to ask the way and, from the instruction I received, was certain of finding my way home. However, rain and the falling darkness drove me along byways to a handsome Manor. After having been exposed to attack by an abundance of Dogs, 16–20 Slaves came forth. They were impertinent enough to refuse to answer me when I asked the way in reasonably good Dutch, despite the fact that some of them certainly understood me, and that I promised them a gratuity; on the contrary, they began discussing among themselves, in broken Portuguese or Malay, in a manner

which made me suspect that these fellow human beings did not harbour any more goodwill toward me than toward any other Foreigners, who are in the habit here of persecuting them; who with both obvious violence and thievery, and with monies, goods, or other things, provide them and their like with the heavy chains they draw. If the master of the house was indeed at home, which I doubt, he would hardly have availed me of any assistance, since such men, living in fear of the vindictiveness of their Slaves, are compelled to securely bolt their doors at night, and keep loaded Rifles at the ready. All the easier, then, for them to both murder me and hide their crime by burying the body, or dragging it deep into the Bushes for the Wild Animals; I therefore proceeded along my way in order to seek a happier fate.

Resa . . ., 1:43–46.

In the Cape Sparrman enjoyed happy days, botanizing, travelling, socializing with the inhabitants of the district, with all different colours and classes. He ran across his colleague and fellow Linnæan disciple Carl Peter Thunberg; they continued botanizing together. He was diligent, eager, cheerful, and generous. But, most of all, he was methodical.

In the beginning almost every day was a rich harvest of the most rare and most beautiful plants for us, when with each new step one or more new discoveries were made. Since many Swedish friends and especially the great Linnæus are always in my thoughts, I even felt a joy within, for each and every duplicate and triplicate &c. of those herbs I plucked; I was, however, not seldom deceived by my greediness by collecting, for myself and my friends, more than I had the time to care for and dry, as one ought. This must happen to more or less every travelling Botanist.

Resa . . ., 1:22.

Sparrman seems not to have looked for adventure, but it seems to have found him anyway. He is stoically self-contained, thereby differing from

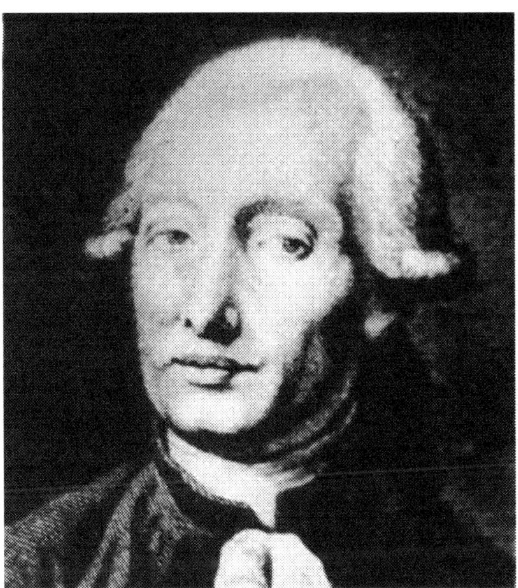

Anders Sparrman travelled with James Cook on his second journey around the world.

the tellers of feats and adventures in the nineteenth century. He differs also in his style, which is packed with humour and self-ironic distance.

I took the road to the right, which was to lead me to a rich and ailing Widow. My Servant, who was known there, warned me not to frighten the Missus with the Insects attached to the brim of my hat, causing me, upon arriving at her home at 5 o'clock and being well received, to carefully turn it inside out, hiding it from her sight in a corner. My mouth was then immediately employed with Cheese, Butter, Bread, Wine, Tea-water, and discussions of the Gout, Stroke, heavy Nosebleed, Cough, and her late Husband's Dropsy; the Old Girl was as anxious to listen as I was to eat, at least as much as my lectures allowed. During this time a gossipy Favorite Slave had spied upon my Servant in the kitchen, wherewith she whispered in the Missus' ear that my hat was full of small Beasts [kleine Bestjes]. The Old Girl immediately broke off the admirable instructions on Diet, which I was in the midst of

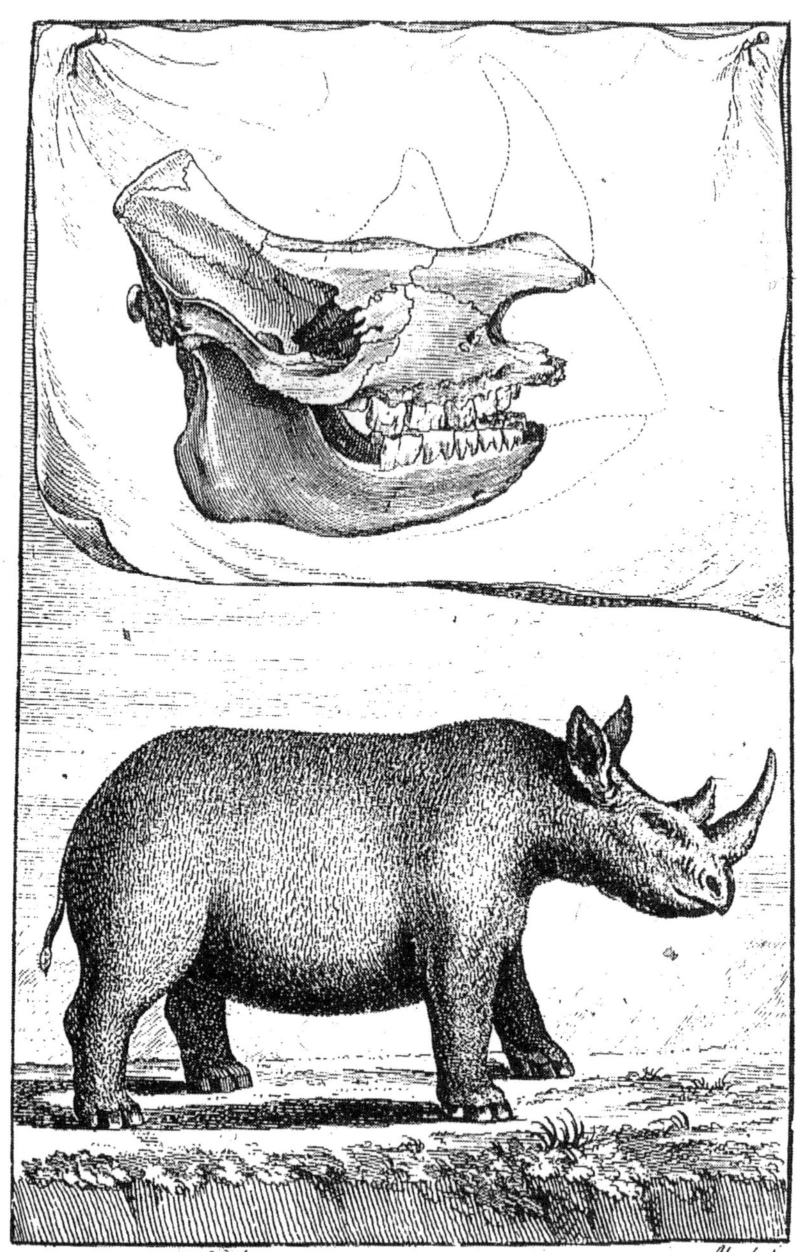

Rhinoceros bicornis. Akrel Sc.

Illustration from Sparrman, A Voyage . . .

providing, in order that she might see the remarkable sights in my hat. She displayed the greatest consternation at seeing the little Beasts nailed to the brim of my hat with pins. An immediate explanation was demanded. I now needed declare a short truce with the victuals, so as not to swallow any of the Dutch Phrases I needed to forge in order to convince her of the benefit knowledge of these small Beasts would have for medicine, Economics, and the glory of the Creator. Successfully, though not without a certain inquietude, I dealt with this subject; for had I not been successful the Missus would surely have shown me the door, accused of being a Magician [Häxemeester]. Now the honourable Old Girl bade me stay, and I looked forward to a delicate night's rest in that beautiful and well-stocked house.

Resa . . . , 1:70–71.

On another occasion Sparrman ends up at the home of a man originally from Hanover, who tells him animated tales about his love life.

He also dictated, in order of preference, a list based securely on long experience of love-making, to wit: Madagaskans, blackest and most splendid, followed by Malabarians, Bugunesians or Malaysians, thereafter Hottentotts, but the very worst, White Dutch women.

Resa . . . , 1:80.

The German had a dozen or so male slaves, which is why the door was securely bolted and five rifles hung close at hand. Sparrman attempted to say that lenience in their treatment was the best way to assure himself of security, but the German turned him a deaf ear. Sparrman also felt that the lonely single men should be allowed to have women slaves with them; it would be more humane. And he concludes that the prosperity of the slave owner was not worth its price.

. . . even the most tolerable Tyranny brings about its own punishment, disturbing both sleep and conscience. Slaves, even under the mildest Tyrant, are deprived of their natural rights; the melancholy thought of such a painful loss is easily awoken in the silence of the night. What wonder then if the perpetrators of this outrage upon their freedom are sometimes compelled to once again sign and seal the Rights of Man with their blood? Ought not my otherwise gentle Host fear the desperation of 12 hale and hearty Men, kidnapped from their land, their families, and their freedom? Cut off from a Sex, which so sweetens our lives, would indeed be terrible, so that their passions, fiery by nature, would attack mankind.

Resa . . . , 1:81–82.

It was during his youthful travels that Sparrman became conscious of injustice. He meets the world with the vulnerable gaze of one with an unclouded sense of fairness. He becomes an abolitionist and allies himself with opinion that has been swelling up primarily in England. For the rest of his life he would fight for the oppressed. Where did such feelings come from? From science? Or was it because of those very feelings that the scientific community eventually did not want anything to do with him?

WITH CAPTAIN COOK

Half a year after Sparrman's arrival at the Cape, Captain Cook's ships *Resolution* and *Adventure* anchored at Taffel-Bayen. As a disciple of the great Linnæus, Sparrman was a much-coveted collaborator on any scientific expedition. Sure enough, he was soon approached by the German father-and-son research team Johann Reinhold and Georg Forster, the latter of whom was also a draughtsman and painter. They asked if he would care to join them on their journey, the main goal being to search for the mystical Southern Continent, the existence of which was still unsubstantiated. Their query had a revolutionary effect upon him.

> I spent the night deep in thought, more disquieted perhaps than one might imagine. In the morning, at the first light of dawn, irresolution drove me to the window of my chambers; I cast my eyes over the surrounding plains, as if I wanted to ask its Flowers if I ought to part from them so hastily. For a long time they had been almost my only joy, Friends, and company; they were that still, which was the greatest force dissuading me from taking that Sea journey. Finally I reached the decision that I should undertake same, but with the firm intention that, after a successful return, I would busy myself anew with the enjoyable research of Nature.
>
> *Resa* . . . , 1:87–80.

One of his farewell letters was addressed to his brother-in-arms, Thunberg.

> Receive here heartfelt and a thousandfold thanksgivings for all the friendship you have shown me on both Swedish and African soil; particularly the friendship you have shown me here, Sir, appears more than sensible in my current undertakings, which when my Friend receives this are already well underway. It is an enterprise the likes of which could well benefit from the advice of so forthright a friend as you, Sir; but you have certainly already heard that I have gone away to the South Pole and onward around the world with the English; what do you think of that, Sir? I will receive your answer only after 2 years have passed, if the South Pole does not become my grave. . .I must. . .briefly name the reasons which induced me to undertake this enterprise; for the first, to Botanize with a Maître d'Ecole is like going to a dinner party and gnawing the bones; heavily hangs the dust of the schoolroom over one . . . Furthermore, I can learn drawing, and English &c. There surely ought be some place in India in need of a Botanist . . . I am now 24 years, so there is still enough time left for me to spend some of it in India if the Good Lord so chooses to dispose, and should I sail back to England so be it . . .

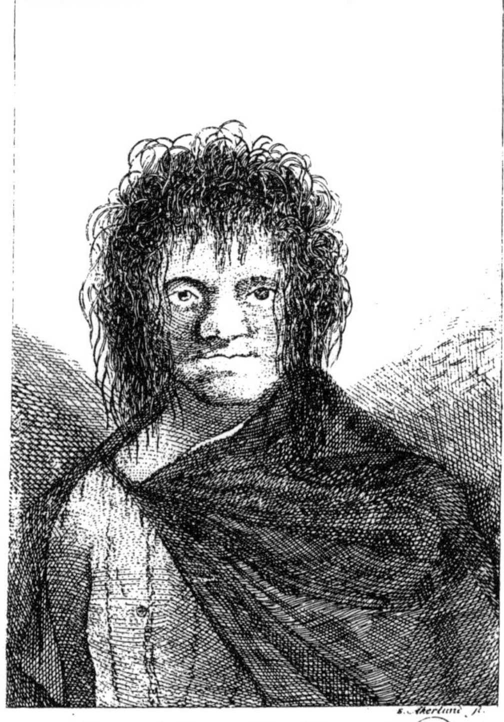

A man from Fuegia. Illustration from Sparrman, A Voyage . . .

He states that he has no cause to complain about his prospects. His travelling companions, the Messrs. Forster, seem to be honourable men who offer him the same comfort they themselves enjoy. The captain, James Cook, was not very well known at the time; Sparrman speaks of him as a "rather honourable man with whom Solander travelled." However, nothing can prevent a feeling of loss and sorrow from bursting forth. It is as if Sparrman thought that the words themselves would exist in time and return to him as comfort in the loneliness of the Polar Sea — or some other place.

> Mon adieu then dearest Friend God bless us and grant us the chance to Botanize together again, if not soon then in those Elysian Fields. May heaven support your endeavours to your pleasure and advantage, wishes a sincere Friend,
>
> Anders Sparrman
>
> Sparrman to Carl Peter Thunberg, Caput B Spei [Cape of Good Hope], Novembris 1772.

The journey was conducted in three "campaigns" in the Antarctic Sea; in between these forays, they set up winter quarters in New Zealand, or travelled the tropical islands in the Pacific Ocean. One of the results of the trip was the conclusion that the Southern Continent, much discussed for many centuries, was unlikely to exist — if it did, it was freezing and unsuitable for human inhabitation. Among the icebergs of the Polar Sea, Sparrman is both a keen observer and a straightforward narrator. He shares his rapture with us.

> On Dec. 11th we first discovered the snow-white, black-beaked Fulmar, the size of a dove, which we learned during the course of our travels was the harbinger and companion of larger amounts of ice. On the other hand, the number of other species of birds seemed to diminish. On the 12th, under thick, hazy air, a journey was made between six mountainous ice masses, of which one was shaded snow-white and transparently crystal clear and sapphire &c., of up to 2 miles' width and 60 feet's height; notwithstanding this height, this iceberg would repeatedly and often disappear under the green ocean waves which crashed furiously against it. Up against the light of a beautiful day, this comprised the most majestic and imposing spectacle on land or sea that I have ever witnessed or believe that nature is generally capable of producing. At the same time it was most terrible, as we ought to bear in mind, how we in darkness, fog, storms, and the swelling seas &c. in such places run the risk of turning from spectators into actors thrown upon that horrible stage; that the highest ship's mast or the frailest human bone can be crushed to bits and wrecked. One can therefore easily imagine how careful we were, especially in darkness and heavy fog, to keep a good watch, and to mind coming too close to the windward side of these ice masses. Numerous whalefish now appeared and provided a little, though no more pleasant, variation among the terrifying icy scenery.
>
> *Resa...*, II:1, 22–23.

During the southern hemisphere's summer, the party forges farther south. Christmas Eve is celebrated at latitude 56 degrees south, with porter, arrack, and bordeaux wines, of which the entire higher command partook so richly, according to Sparrman, "that a few of us with a more than ordinary philosophical sobriety viewed the ice and dangers of the day and the journey." The crew got drunk on its increased Christmas rum rations, and boxing matches were arranged on deck. There is an arch, sometimes slightly comical tone in Sparrman's description, but he considered it objective. In fact, he defends his style and his choice of facts against the evidence provided by others.

> My painting... [of the first polar campaign], far from being embellished (or as one usually says, artificial), is, in the liveliness of the colours rather, and naturally so, duller than nature's own; but my drawing is nonetheless measured with the greatest care with the yardstick of truth. Far from wanting to let Penguins dance, or run on top of the water, I have been careful to allow nature and truth to wander in their own naturally simple way, and believe our campaign to be remarkable enough that it deserves the sacrifice of prolixity in its description.
>
> *Resa...*, II:1, 53.

PARADISE ISLANDS AND MAN-EATERS

Sparrman's account returns to slavery, oppression, and cannibalism at times during the trip. It seems as if the subject never really lets him go. In

Tahiti, once an isle of paradise, ruin had already set in since the advent of the Europeans. In the native upper classes Sparrman sees a brutal aristocracy that easily matched its European counterpart in gluttony and lechery, though outdid it in its horrifying custom of murdering children and practicing human sacrifice. In New Zealand, he is led to believe that the Maori are cannibals, which makes him unfavourably disposed toward that country.

> At any rate, one should not expect any great nation to emerge from the undelightful climate of man-eaters, where jealousy, hate, and rapacity are the Primitive's natural siblings, alongside a deep-seated, horrific taste for blood-letting and eating the flesh of human beings... The same thing can be said of the more northerly-situated of this country's primitives, and, excepting man-eating, I believe that I recognized in the New Zealanders and their wildness, many of the features of our Geatish forefathers, the Vikings, war and murder mandates with both sword and fire and brand, and who knows how much further the frenzy of victory and vengeance drove them toward unnaturalness. We know for a fact that they derived pleasure from drinking out of the skulls of their enemies.
>
> *Resa* ..., II:I, 68 ff.

Thus Sparrman did not rule out the possibility that even the Scandinavians may have once been cannibals. If he exhibits prejudice and conceit, then he does so indiscriminately.

Among the Maori, his fear of cannibals takes on a very special significance, since the custom there was to rub noses when greeting one another.

> I remember well having read in my childhood years that a similar nose-greeting ceremony existed among our more northerly countrymen, the Laplanders; never could I have imagined that I myself, many times, would exercise the same method of greeting in New Zealand! My nose so often and so close to the teeth of a man-eater and yet so near to Sweden, this is truly often both a ridiculous and consoling thought.
>
> *Resa* ..., II:I, 72.

Sparrman seems to have become "Anglicized" during his trip around the world. From the end of the 1770s his letters are filled with English formulations, sometimes changing language in the middle of a sentence. In the autumn of 1776 he travels to London in order to visit the collections there; he has now decided to do something with the specimens and ethnographic material he has gathered on his journey — to the great delight of the Academy of Sciences in Stockholm.

> The Secretary stated having met Doctor Sparrman in Gothenburg, recently returned from his journey to *Caput Bonæ Spei* and around the Antarctic Circle, and having seen some of the collections made by him there, which were quite substantial and remarkable. Doctor Sparrman said he was of a mind to send the greater part of them by sea from Gothenburg to Stockholm, from which plan the Secretary dissuaded him, due to the risks, in this late time of the Season. He asked if the Royal Academy could not grant Dr. Sparrman some Sum to send the goods from Gothenburg up here by land, so that such long-travelled and highly rare Natural Specimens should run no risk of being lost, when they have thus far happily come so near... The Royal Academy found this quite necessary, as well as economical to favour and encourage Dr. Sparrman with some support now, after his having made his protracted and extensive Journey without the slightest support from the Royal Academy or the Fatherland. It was therefore decided, unanimously, that he should now immediately receive, to the ends referred, One thousand Thalers, whereof 300 would be sent to him by Post the following day.
>
> Minutes of the Royal Academy of Sciences, September 11, 1776.

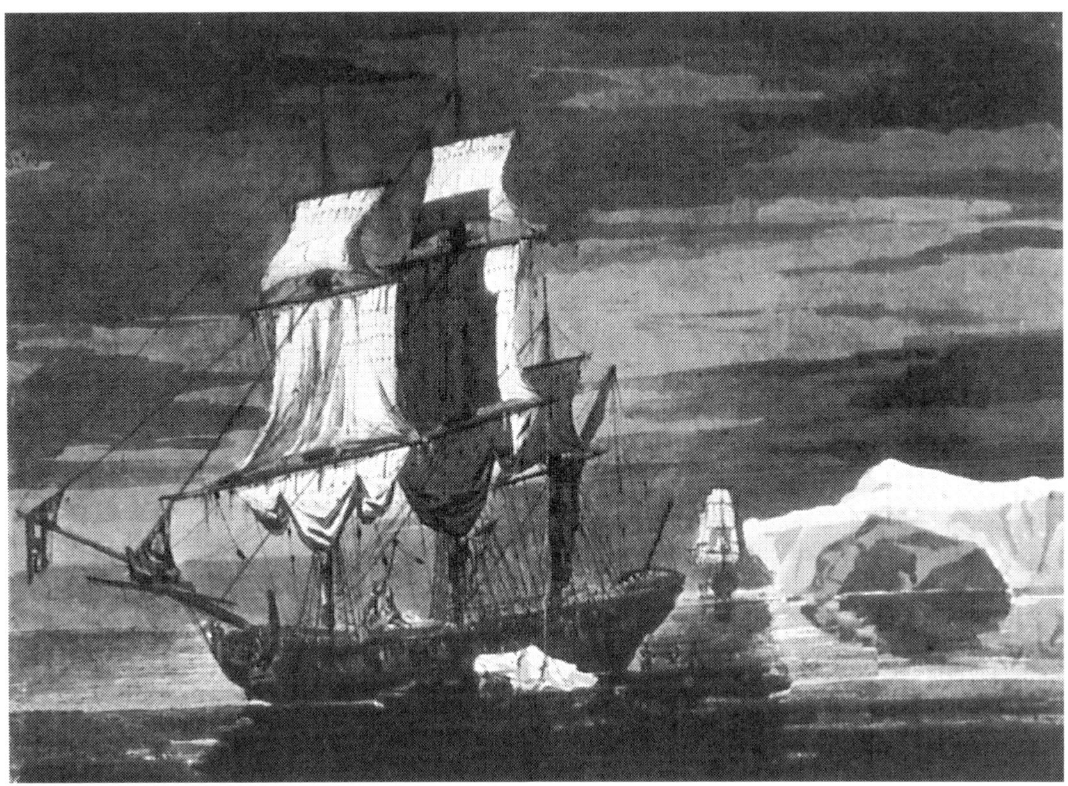

Resolution *and* Adventure *loading ice for water supplies. Aquatint by William Hodges.*

BUREAUCRAT

In addition to his own collections, Sparrman was also to take care of a large donation made by entomologist Charles De Geer. All of this was to be put in order and catalogued for the natural sciences cabinet of the Academy of Sciences, to which he was now attached as curator. His passion still unabated, a thirty-year-old man of vision now set to work. He maintained contact with Claes Alströmer, who sends him books from England. In 1785, an Englishman offers to sell him a particular botanical work, but he cannot take him up on his offer. The reason is lack of funds, a constantly recurring theme throughout his life.

> Poverty forbids me from giving in to my desire to acquire this and many other necessary books of natural history. I must work hard for my living and the necessities of life. A significant portion of my wages go to paying the debts of my beloved old mother, who is seventy-four, and who beggered herself by offering her children an education... Many a time, my lord, would I have had to suffer seeing my entire family go under before my very eyes had I not through my toiling as a physician been able to keep us above the surface (if but barely). In order to achieve that goal, I have been forced to waste my time on common surgery, time I had

> much rather, my lord, and with greater results, dedicated to the study of natural history... The height of my fortune in my native country is a pension of 100 thalers, or 24 pounds sterling per annum from our Royal Academy of Sciences, I am, in other words, paid the same amount as the footman at the above-named academy. In addition, the footman is provided with free living quarters whilst I must pay 33 thalers for my rooms...
>
> Sparrman to an anonymous English correspondent, April 25, 1785.

This was, of course, nothing more than a begging letter. It also demonstrates his problematic relationship with the Academy, which he felt refused to pay him what he was worth, and did not fully appreciate his efforts with the collection. The Academy was of quite the opposite opinion: Sparrman was not doing his job properly. He was neglecting his duties to such a degree that in 1784 the Academy reduced his salary to the 100 thalers mentioned in the letter. The official motivation was that, through the donations of De Geer and Sparrman, the collections were now in order. At the same time, the Academy issued instructions to the curator, which in detail and rather caustically described what he ought to be doing.

> 3. The Demonstrator... ought also to dust the Birds and Quadrupeds, which are not protected from Moths by Glass, as well as exposing them a number of times to the open Air in the Summertime, and also if necessary, rid them of Moths with Smokelamps, if they are seen to be so afflicted. He ought also to remember to preserve them from Moths by applying proper amounts of sublimate, or some other suitable substance.
>
> 4. The Royal Academy entrusts the Curator with the reasonable task of, in all possible ways, attempting to enlarge this collection of natural specimens, which is also expected of all of its members, whenever they are able. But the Academy particularly expects that the Curator see it as a duty to procure all the known Insects of Sweden, and herbs, and even minerals, so that a Swedish Academy of Sciences may be able to display Swedish natural historical specimens.
>
> "Proposal to an Instruction to the Curator of the Museum of the Royal Academy of Sciences," February 18, 1783.

Being issued such exacting instructions after five years of service was not a good sign, and Sparrman fought back the best he could. In a memo, he detailed how much he had done for the museum.

> ...thus in the arrangement of the specimens according to their correct name, Genera and Species it has been necessary to lift and handle, sometimes several times, many hundredfold Animals and beasts, in order to e.g. count the number of rays and gills on the fishes, plus the *scuta* and *Sqvamae* of over 150 Snakes... Through various friendships, correspondence, and the exchanging of duplicates, I have considered it a delightful duty, without any cost to the Academy, to enlarge its Collection; accordingly, Herr Director Suther donated... the Cedar chest containing Birds and splendid Butterflies, for which, as I happen to know, he paid an Officer from Surinam over 60 Ducats; and, for the same reasons, Herr Director Staaf writes on 16th Oct. 1782 that he makes a present to the Academy of his Chinese *Materia Medica* in 500 tin boxes including lids, and for which Herr Maul paid 120 piasters in Canton. The *Gorgonia Spiralis* of unmatched size and the Orang-outan, which I have secured free of charge through my former shipmate Herr Captain Burtz, would undeniably bring in between 12 and 15 ducats a piece from connoisseurs at an auction in Holland...
>
> Sparrman memo, February 4, 1784.

Sparrman was provided with a flat oin the Academy's premises on Stora Nygatan. Just a few feet away stood the stuffed animals, the bottles with their preparations, the heavy mineral cabinets, all housed in their own room. In

Sparrman's quarters there hung a portrait of Linnæus. Twice Sparrman was named president of the Academy, a highly meritorious post. Occasionally he took sabbaticals, once in order to travel to West Africa. It is perhaps typical of him that he officially reported that he was travelling to take the waters at a spa. The collections he was responsible for were not large. A visitor to the museum wrote in his diary in 1789:

> [Here one finds] the head of a buffalo, a young seahorse, a piece of inch-thick elephant skin and one of its teeth, weighing 100 pounds, the horn of a rhinoceros, the head of a Babyrusae swine, Tahitian tapestries, clothing, axes, weapons, and Japanese cups, some birds, many seashells, insects, fishes, lizards, snakes.

In 1798, the Academy appointed a demonstrator, whose job was to reinvigorate the collection. Sparrman could only interpret this as repudiation, which in fact it was, and he resigned permanently from his post in order to dedicate himself more seriously to the occult phenomena which were beginning to take up more and more of his time. Less significantly, he began to also display a certain distaste for meat. Commenting on a proposal to include propaganda for horsemeat in the Academy's almanac, he wrote that one ought not "turn our nation more carnivorous than it already is."

STOCKHOLM'S BEST-KNOWN MAGNETIST

Parallel to his image as disciple of Linnæus and increasingly controversial curator of the museum of the Academy of Sciences, a very different picture of Anders Sparrman begins to emerge.

This other image of Sparrman has its basis in his role as a physician. As early as his first trip to East Asia as a seventeen-year-old, he bore the title of field surgeon. After his studies under Linnæus and his long journey, he opened a medical practice to supplement his scanty wages from the Academy.

In those days, doctors fought a hopeless battle against numerous highly prevalent diseases like tuberculosis, dysentery, plague, and cholera epidemics, plus numerous fatal childhood diseases.

These epidemics engendered some questionable efforts at finding effective cures and medicines. One of these so-called cures was to have special meaning for Sparrman. It is a phenomenon which also had significance for the followers of Emanuel Swedenborg, dividing their congregations into those who were for it and those who were dead against.

> Animal magnetism is entirely rejected by . . . the congregation in London as in total disagreement with the New Teaching, being only an irritant to Divine Providence in seeking to know that which ought to remain hidden: all of our friends in England are thus inclined . . . to reject magnetism, as is the Society in Stockholm . . . Sparrman is now the greatest magnetist in Stockholm: but he is far from being a true Swedenborgian, and will never be; but since he is a foolish man without system or acuteness of Perception, it behooves us to forgive him . . .
>
> C.F. Bergklint to unknown lieutenant-colonel, March 4, 1771.

Magnetism had become the fashionable cure among the upper classes in Europe, and it rapidly gained a foothold in Stockholm.

According to the theory of Franz Anton Mesmer, the life and health of all living beings was influenced by a magnetic flow which saturated the cosmos. The significance and utilization of this magnetic force was interpreted by different schools of thought. Some, inspired by Swedenborg's theory of spirits, saw an opportunity to

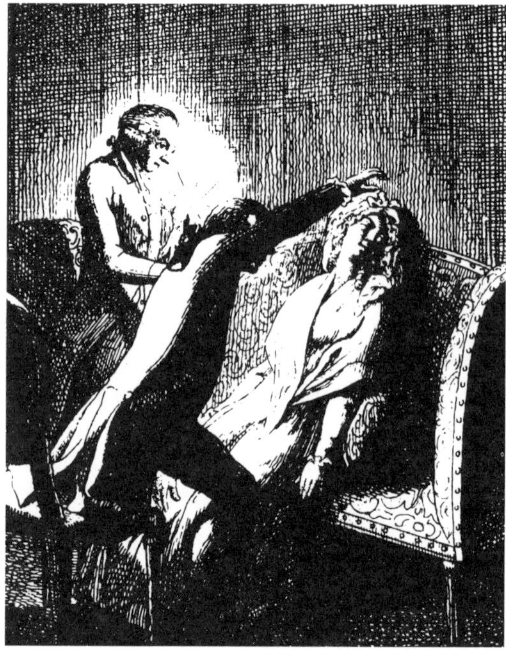

Mesmerizing a lady.

experiment at making contact with the spirits of the dead, a way of imitating Swedenborg's own contact with the other side. Others saw the magnetic flow as more of a physical force, a force with miraculous healing powers.

In Anders Sparrman's personal interpretation of animal magnetism, faith in a spiritual force dominates. His anonymously published *Om prest-medicin och animal magnetism* constantly refers to magnetism as "the fluidum of Christianity," as a means of both making contact with the spirits and curing the sick.

> I hereby have the honour of personally presenting you, via the post, with a copy of "Priest-Medicine and Magnetism." The other 4 enclosed are for sale at a price of 12 thalers each ... though I do not wish to be identified as the author. Magnetism is no doubt such an unknown Science in Uppsala that those four will probably remain unsold, but should the Bookseller there require them then I shall send more copies through you.
>
> Sparrman to Carl Peter Thunberg, undated.

The magnetists came under devastating fire from both the Enlightenment and the Church, which together sank the movement. Once again, Sparrman exhibits a distinct independence, or obstinacy, if you will. He never lost faith in magnetism and never stopped defending his unpopular opinions.

> There was so much teasing and defaming of magnetism in company that I finally felt called upon to prove in black and white their prejudices; what they had not understood they experienced as anti-magnetistic nonsense — Among them Berzelius, with his Chemical arrogance and medical ignorance, and Odhelius, with his intolerance. Hagström believes whatever Hufeland does, as does Trafvenfelt. By reading the Journal, Hedin is now converted.
>
> Sparrman to Carl Peter Thunberg, September 14, 1815.

BACK TO AFRICA

During the 1780s, Sparrman met two Swedenborgians who were to exert a lasting influence on the latter part of his life. One of them was Carl Bernhard Wadström — inventor, factory owner, abolitionist, a man who at the time of his death in 1799 in revolutionary France had received honourary French citizenship. The other was August Nordenskjöld, alchemist and utopian.

Together with Wadström and the chemist Arrhenius, Anders Sparrman embarks on a new, long journey, this time to West Africa. It is a strange trip, surrounded by great secrecy. After his return to Sweden he writes:

> The reason for my Trip to Gorée and Senegal is the secret which died with Gustavus III and Louis XVI, but a little story about aforesaid Trip has been published in England by Director-General Wadström and has been translated into Swedish.
>
> Sparrman to unnamed Swedish deputy judge.

Two different motives may be suggested for the trip:

First, the three men had succeeded in piquing the interest of Gustavus III in establishing a Swedish colony in West Africa, as part of a trade triangle among Sweden, the slave coast, and the new Swedish colony St. Barthélemy in the West Indies. They had even persuaded the king to sponsor their African adventure.

Secondly, Wadström cherished the hope of founding a "New Jerusalem" in the spirit of Swedenborg in the tropics.

Officially, Sparrman had to be granted a leave of absence from the Academy of Sciences, presumably to take the waters at an unnamed spa. This excuse did not stop him from sending a collection of live African birds to the Academy from Senegal.

Sparrman, along with Wadström, had become engaged in the Utopia of the Swedenborgians. Africa was chosen as their destination because of Swedenborg's idea that the interior of Africa was a site of hibernation for primitive Christianity, a place which had preserved traditions from the time of Jesus and the apostles. The right spot from which to approach this apostolic heritage was, according to the Master, the western coast of the continent.

After Wadström had made contact with primitive Christianity, he and Nordenskjöld wanted to found a New Jerusalem, a "Republique of God," where power would rest in the hands of the workers and where the supremacy of money would meet its demise. Nordenskjöld had plans and dreams embracing all humanity. He would break the domination of capital through his own energetic contributions as an alchemist. In his alchemical efforts, Nordenskjöld was driven not by prospects of infinite personal riches but by burning conviction.

Through alchemy, he intended to reduce gold to the ranks of one metal among many others, thereby creating chaos in an economy based on the gold standard. "Within a few years," he confidently reports in an alchemical work from 1779, "money will be like dross."

His contemporaries were not certain that this was completely out of the question. Hedging his bets, Gustavus III provided Nordenskjöld with a laboratory at the royal palace Drottningholm.

> Wadström's and my own testimony in London for a Committee of the Upper Parliament has surely benefitted mankind insofar as concerns the revealing and occurrence of cruelty in the slave trade...
>
> Sparrman to unknown deputy judge.

Even before his voyage, Sparrman was convinced of the reprehensibility of the slave trade, as his earlier writings testify. It is possible that he influenced his companions to openly reject slavery. Certainly, it was a natural standpoint for the freedom-loving Wadström, but, at the beginning of the journey, he has promises to keep to the king and the newly incorporated West India Company, for whom the slave trade was strictly business.

During the West African sojourn, the companions are doubly upset by the barbarity of the colonial powers. Not only did they witness the cruelties on the island of Gorée, where slaves were gathered to wait for the crossing to Ameri-

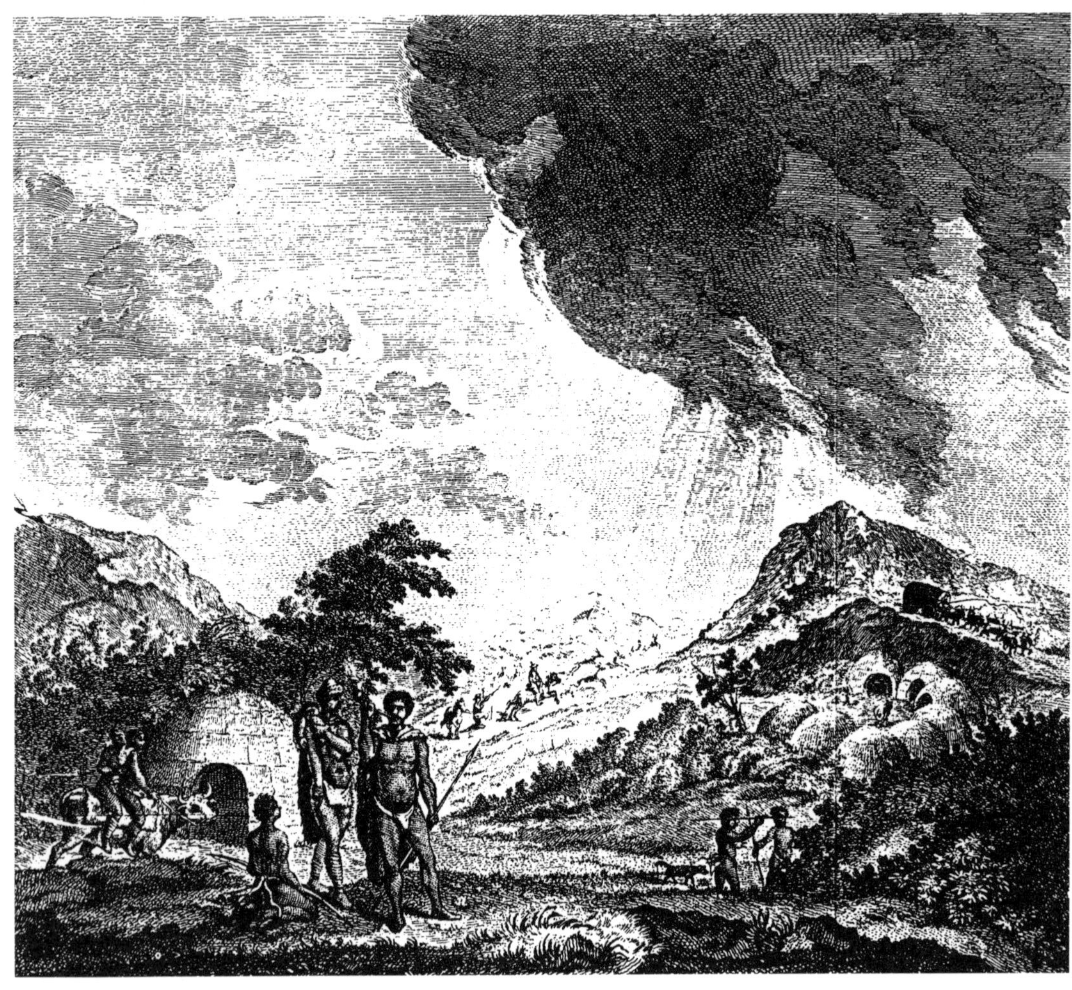

ca, but their own plans were rebuffed by slave traders, whose tentacles stretched over the entire western coast of Africa. The road was blocked for the Swedes, and after only a few months they were back in Europe.

In September 1789, Sparrman writes:

> I have received Observations on the Slave Trade, on top of all the other material on that subject which I have already acquired (pretty soon an entire Library) from the Society for Abolishing. A large folio is supposed to have recently been published containing all the testimony on this topic, among them Wadström's and mine on provisioning the slaveships with poisons with which to slay the slaves, in the event of headwinds and lack of water, as so often happens...

Sparrman to unnamed Swedish professor, September 29, 1789.

We do not know the extent of the role Sparrman had in this infatuation with Africa. Without a doubt, the Swedenborgians played the leading parts. What we do know is that the mysterious expedition to West Africa would be Sparrman's last long trip. After delivering his testimony against the slave trade to the House of Lords, he heads back home.

"A CAREER IN DECLINE"

Around the turn of the century, Anders Sparrman was still numbered among the scientific nobility in Sweden. In a series of caricatures of famous Swedes, with which the Italian traveller Giuseppe Acerbi spiced up his Swedish travelogue, we find the following. It begins with a mention of Sparrman's magnetist activities:

> Herr Sparrman, physician and one of the "Illuminated" or Mesmer's disciples. His name is occasionally seen in connection with the renowned Captain Cook's, despite the fact that he had nothing more to do with him than sail in the same ship. Herr Sparrman has made a name for himself with his *Voyage to the Cape of Good Hope*, which is a feeble work. Furthermore, he has published a number of other books and dissertations which do not entitle him to a particularly high stature in the republic of science. I have also heard that the Academy's museum had earlier been in his care, but that he has been succeeded at this post by Dr. Quenzel.
>
> Giuseppe Acerbi, *Travels through Sweden, Finland and Lapland to the North Cape, in the Years 1798 and 1799.*

Anders Sparrman would remain a bachelor throughout his life. In appreciation for the exhibits he donated, including a foal of the now extinct South African quagga (a rarity which can still be seen today at the Museum of Natural History in Stockholm), he was allowed to live, in a tiny "academic exception," in the museum — where one imagines he had plenty of opportunity to gnash his teeth over the excellent job his successor, Quenzel, was doing.

Sparrman was not suited to academic life. He succeeded in being fired not only from his job at the museum but from his professorship in natural history, and he later resigned his chair in surgery at the Karolinska Institute. He is described as careless and impractical. In the curt assessments of historians he emerges as a failure, "a disharmonious person," "a career in decline," "died destitute." What is mysterious about Sparrman's being an outsider is that he himself chose that role.

One of the few academic friends who stood by him to the bitter end was Thunberg. Since their youthful days botanizing together in the Cape, the two had always kept in touch. The majority of Sparrman's letters that have been preserved are to Thunberg, addressed in the fashion of the day as "Honoured Herr Professor and Knight of the Order of Wasa." Thunberg attempts to persuade Sparrman to apply for a professorship in economics at Uppsala in his old age, to which Sparrman replies:

> My Worthiest Friend!
> Tout considéré, I dare not seek the Chair both for fear of receiving it and not receiving it! Being turned down is tedious, and to be married to that old maid Economics and to Teach new Lessons with her would be boring...my practice is both successful and boring, but I am light on my feet both on the stairs and in the street, am invested with much faith and derive Satisfaction by doing useful things at the sickbed after long experience and extensive daily reading of new things and old, which also interest me for the sake of execrating my own ailing body and those of my Friends. Holidays from an academy, on the other hand, would

> be interesting and would be put to use in travelling through the whole of Sweden, if I had the money and high enough wages to do it ... Here, I have the practical perquisites of shoe-repair and tailoring from patients. Buns from the Baker and ... Meat from the Butcher, a better variety of fish ... A bunch of acquaintances to visit and go out with at times — I am closer to the wellspring of news and announcements ... If I manage to live a little longer I hope to be granted a Medical Counselor's pension. If I die, then I die — with honour!
>
> Sparrman to Carl Peter Thunberg, May 24, 1815.

After the turn of the century, Sparrman was no longer referred to as a practising magnetist, a profession at which he apparently did not celebrate much success. On the contrary, he suffered clear failures, among them the lady-in-waiting Charlotte Eckerman, who, according to reports, "was magnetized to death by Professor Sparrman" in the 1780s. In later years, Sparrman seems to have contented himself with studying magnetism in theory.

There were spiritistic elements in his magnetistic activities, but his interpretation of the possibilities of animal magnetism was both moving and oddly related to modern theories of health care. It concerned a holistic perception of the sick person and wished to mobilize all the person's resources in the struggle against pain. A conviction Sparrman maintained throughout his life was that united, spiritual and physical forces could accomplish amazing things.

We know very little about his life outside the scientific sphere. In fragments of letters, he airs some of his thoughts. A letter to his friend Thunberg from this time contains a lovely but opaque commentary on some adventure.

> P.S. It remained for me to once again try my luck against the caprices of Fortune, that unstable goddess, and show her the spear, and defy her divine power. I shall never forget that She, the very one, rests on a sphere, but never on a Square stone, and that she, glorious in memory, often takes everything from us — except the shadow of our former prosperity. Had I known her intrigues, and the secret passageways which carry the sacrifices to her sacrificial altar, had I known 20 years ago, I'd have caught up with her, but now I have also grown old, and soon, will hardly have the strength to walk, let alone catch up with her at a full career. And without being at all jealous, I gladly leave that to her slaves. From now on I shall always look upon her physiognomy with cold contempt, and teach her to respect a bold countenance. Joy! o Joy! for our Masculine Genus that she brands her own weak Sex, and I pass over her other merits in silence, since she is as old as the earth itself.
>
> Sparrman to Carl Peter Thunberg, January 29, 1809.

TARDY TRAVELOGUE

Aside from his physician's practice and his interest in magnetism, Sparrman also cultivated the heritage of Linnæus, if in his own very personal way. The latter two parts of his writings from his long journey of the 1770s were finally published, the last of them in 1818. By then, forty-two years had passed since the celebrated traveller had come home from his journeys — a singular record in tardiness.

His interest in ornithology manifests itself in several publications, among them a stately collection of prints from the bird cabinet of Gustaf von Carlsson — one hundred exotic species, including some never previously described.

During his last fifteen years, he worked periodically on the never-completed *Swedish Ornithology*. The work was published, plate by plate, up until 1816, when his health finally failed him. The text breaks off in the middle of his description of the golden oriole.

The figure of Anders Sparrman remains mysterious and ambiguous on many important levels. How could there be room for enlightenment and occultism, the heritage of Linnæus and Mesmeric spiritism, in one and the same soul? We do not know the answer, but a better illustration of the transitional period between the Enlightenment and Romanticism is hard to find. And in the end, perhaps it was no more difficult for him to create a coherent worldview of these contrasting aspects than it is for people of our own age to deal with contemporary contradictions.

Anders Sparrman's last days were said to have been spent in grief and misery. His reputation as the most widely travelled of the disciples of Linnæus, which once won him a place in the academies, was not enough to protect him after he turned his back on the institutions. The glory of his voyage of discovery with Captain Cook had long since lost its lustre. At the time of his death in 1820, there were probably only a few who attached any importance to the fact that Anders Sparrman remained the person who had been farthest south on the planet.

Having approached the Ice as near as we dared, and thus begun to turn the ship Northwards thence, I, in order to avoid the usual hubbub and crush such manoeuvres caused on deck, went below to the cabin to quietly view the endless arctic ice-theatre from its windows. In this manner did it occur, as my travelling companions noted, that I had come a little bit more south than any of the others on board, since a ship when turning always drops slightly astern before it can pick up speed on a new tack by filling its sails.

Resa . . ., II:2, 48.

Translated from the Swedish by Stephen Fruitman

OTTO FAGERSTEDT is executive producer of the Documentary Department of the Swedish Broadcasting Corporation. SVERKER SÖRLIN is a historian of science and holds the chair of environmental history at the University of Umeå. In Artes no. 1, 1994, the authors contributed an essay on the travels of Linnæus and his disciples. STEPHEN FRUITMAN, born in Canada, is a graduate student in the Department of History of Science and Ideas at the University of Umeå.

The Garden

MAGNUS FLORIN

Behind the Linnæus of this story stands Carl von Linné (1707–1778). Herein are reflections of the great naturalist's works and of the garden at Hammarby and the surrounding countryside, but "The Garden" is not intended as a documentary. It is a fantasy.

It is muddy autumn. It is not warm, not cold. The gardener feels the soil between his thumb and middle finger. He smells it, tastes it. It is the salt sea. It is the black clay of the Uppsala plain. He strolls, as he is in the habit of doing, round the squares of the plant beds. He rakes dry leaves from the paths. He puts the rake in the toolshed and falls asleep inside, waiting. He is woken by a cloudburst. It is Thursday morning and time for the cheese and butter delivery from Hallkved.

The gardener exchanges a few words with the coachman and the farmhand, who are soaked by the driving rain. They laugh together. They yawn. They stand silent, looking out over the plain, the clay, and over towards the cornfields.

They think about porridge, gruel, bread.

They stand silent, still. It is a long drawn-out moment.

But a shift comes and the two of them show signs of departing, take their places in the cart and journey on towards Lövsta.

The gardener stands with the butter and cheese in his arms and looks after them. Then he goes in the direction of the underground food-cellar.

*

Linnæus is out in the wind on the Uppsala plain, waiting for the vehicle from the coaching establishment at Böksta. Linnæus is in his chamber dressing.

Now, if you are Linnæus, you are to be Linnæus.

Clearly Linnæus buttons up the twenty-five buttonholes in his waistcoat with his own fingers. He fastens the buttons with the thumbs, index fingers, and middle fingers of both hands, and is careful not to fasten them unevenly. He can begin from the top or the bottom — in this he allows himself a bit of variety — but never in the middle. Beginning in the middle is only advisable with shirts, which never have more than seventeen buttons, but even with them he finds it more convenient to begin from the bottom or the top. In fact, he usually sets about it from the top, for the simple reason that it is difficult to see the lower buttonholes and buttons in the mirror.

Now he is fastening the twenty-eight buttons in the long green camlet coat and taking care not to fasten them unevenly.

Now he tosses up the twenty-five and the twenty-eight buttonholes high above his head and he will not get them back.

Now, if you must be Linnæus.

Linnæus is out in the wind on the Uppsala plain, waiting to set off, with his large bag in his hand.

He lifts the bag high in the air: take this bag! But nobody takes the bag out of his hands and he remains standing. The wind blows and he feels it blowing.

But now he tosses up the twenty-eight youths, the twenty-eight disciples, into the wind on the Uppsala plain, and they are scattered.

*

In this world, Linnæus is at home. He searches, all by himself, for an important passage in a work in progress simply to give himself a pretext for perusing each sheet of paper. He directs shrieks of dissatisfaction at his writing materials. He walks up and down in irritation. He drums on the desk with his fingers. He flings himself on the bed, snorting.

These are all regular affectations. Actually he is content. Often he needs only to linger a little by the glass panes of the cabinets and to gaze at the vessels behind them to feel at peace.

But today that is not enough. There is a stirring of unease in his body.

He goes into the instrument room and over to the window that looks out onto the garden. It is his garden, which he has laid out. Beside the window, close by the frame, he has placed a map of the garden. "Plan" would perhaps be a more accurate word. He sees, and rejoices over, the congruity between the garden in the picture and the real garden.

The gardener is moving about outside, this way and that, to and fro. It seems arbitrary. Occasionally he falls over, but gets up again immediately. He struggles forward, as if into a headwind. He walks with a firm stride, then suddenly staggers and falls headlong, or chooses a new direction and walks on.

Linnæus pulls a face behind the windowpane, waves, and tries to attract the gardener's attention with a "Halloo!" He wants the gardener to stop, perhaps take a break, pull off his shoes and see to his toes and the soles of his feet, as he usually does. But the gardener carries on.

Linnæus thinks: his continual, everlasting motion!

Now there is a ceremony or show, as if in a salon. First figure: *le pantalon.* Then *l'été.* Third figure: *la poule.* After that *la pastourelle.* Finally the fifth figure: *le final.*

Linnæus finds this admirable. A round of applause would be in order. But the gardener dances on into something else. Linnæus remains standing at the window and watches a strange ballet, quite absurd.

The windowpane is dirty. It has been cleaned recently, but the dirt has not been removed and in the process of rinsing it has dried out in the pattern of a wave. It has an unexpectedly artistic appearance. Linnæus gazes at it. When he looks out again, the gardener is gone.

*

"Take this rake," the gardener says to Linnæus.

Linnæus tries to take it.

"Not like that," says the gardener. He means: "Take it, take it as an idea. Think about it."

But Linnæus cannot think about the rake as an idea. There are so many rakes and so many kinds of rake. Quite definitely one must think of a particular kind of rake: a hayrake, for example, of a particular shape.

The gardener stares hard at Linnæus and says it is a matter of this very rake, a rake which must be perceived as a quite definite rake of a quite definite type.

Linnæus says that he is thinking of this rake.

The gardener asks if he is quite sure about that.

Linnæus answers in the affirmative.

The gardener says that Linnæus is to take the rake, yes, really take it in his hand and start raking.

Linnæus does this and rakes away some leaves and some blades of grass from the path. What a lot of leaves and grass there are here, he thinks.

The gardener asks if Linnæus is still thinking about the rake while he is raking. Linnæus says he cannot do that. He has to rake.

Then the gardener says: "There is a difference."

Linnæus asks: "What difference?"

"That," says the gardener, "is the difference."

*

It is dawn, on the 28th of January. Carl's name day. The river Sävja is a thin trickle in its bed under the ice this January, when the waxwings gather in the rowans, within easy reach of a shower of hail.

The animals, alarmed, are making themselves scarce. The horses, likewise, take fright.

Linnæus, awake, steps outside, wanders to his grove. He hangs pairs of green Kungsholm glasses as bells on the branches of an oak, an elm, and an ash in order to listen to the jingling caused by the wind when it rises. They are his Aeolian beakers, his wind harps of glass. But this morning the wind is still, and the bells are motionless.

One glass he has saved. He pours wine into it, to the brim, and drains it to celebrate the name of the day.

*

Linnæus makes a distinction between the realm of plants and the realm of animals. But he says there is a third one. It is the realm of stones. In his garden of plants and animals he now wants to have a ring of stone. And therefore tells the gardener to make plans for a stone fence.

The gardener replies that he knows the powers that be have decreed that stone fences are to be erected.

Linnæus says that his stone fence is to be erected for the sake of the garden, not because of enclosure regulations.

The gardener does not reply. He looks down at the ground. Looks out at the fields.

Linnæus says that his stone fence is to lie, not round the garden, but in it.

The gardener asks if Linnæus has seen Bielke's dike at Lövsta. The one that was erected in the autumn of the year before last. And which has already started to fall down.

Linnæus says that he has every confidence in his friend Bielke.

He says: "My highly esteemed friend Sten Carl Bielke, Vice President of His Majesty's Royal Court of Appeal in Åbo, who together with myself founded the Academy of Sciences."

He continues: "Baron Sten Carl Bielke, who along with me introduced the Latin letter form into Swedish scientific writing."

The gardener replies that, in any event, Bielke's stone wall is in a lamentable state.

Linnæus says the gardener is entitled to that opinion and that, whatever the case may be, a stone fence can in all likelihood be erected more or less well.

The gardener replies that a stone fence cannot be well erected at all, since when summer comes it will be destroyed by the sun, which will warm up the south side while the north side is covered in snow and ice, with the result that the stones on the south side will work loose and fall out.

Linnæus says this can be repaired.

The gardener replies that repairs of that kind are more labour-intensive and costly than building. That it would be better to erect a whole new stone fence every year at the end of the summer. That the whole countryside could devote itself to building stone fences all summer long.

Linnæus thinks that he could easily erect a stone fence in his garden himself, all on his own, if only a little one.

☆

The gardener says he can put something in Linnæus's hand which he, Linnæus, will not be able to see, although everybody else in the whole world can see it. Linnæus cannot believe this. The gardener insists he can. Linnæus denies it.

The gardener lifts Linnæus's left hand to his left ear and closes his thumb and index finger round the earlobe. Then he asks: "Can you see your ear?"

Linnæus wants to reply: is it as simple as that? But he says nothing.

The gardener: "Everyone else can see it, but you cannot see it."

The disciple Rolander is in the garden. He asks the gardener if the grass snake is poisonous, if the greenfly bites, if the crow pecks people's eyes out.

When the gardener replies, Rolander leans his head back, gazes intently upwards, and grips his nose with his fingers. The gardener falls silent.

They stand like this for a while. Then Rolander leans forward, blows coagulated blood out of his nostrils, and spits on the ground several times.

☆

It is the 17th of February, late evening. Linnæus and the gardener are out in the waterlogged meadows at Lövsta. Bright moonlight. The forest hard on the horizon.

The almanac shows a minor lunar eclipse at eleven o'clock at night.

The gardener cups his hands, as if to capture something. It is a game. Linnæus guesses.

"Mussels."

Linnæus knows the gardener maintains that he has found the mollusc shells in the clay. Shells of molluscs from the salty Baltic, which stretched this far until the land rose.

Linnæus specifies: "*Mytilus edulis,* the common sea mussel. *Cardium edule,* the cockle, with its ribbed shell. *Tellina baltica,* the little smooth one."

"Feel," says the gardener, lifting up a handful of soil to Linnæus , who takes it. "Feel!"

Linnæus rubs the soil between his fingers, the black, smooth, clay soil, blank in the white light. He says nothing.

The gardener peeps at him: "There are bullheads and turbot out here."

A little shadow passes over the edge of the moon.

"The peasants say we are out in the bay now."

The shadow over the side of the moon slowly disappears. Linnæus thinks that soon they will be rowing home.

*

Wind. The gardener and Linnæus are standing in the grove beside the oak, the elm and the ash, listening to the jingling of the Aeolian bells.

"Glass," says the gardener, "as a material is fluid in its natural state. At our temperature it takes on a more solid form. But it is still fluid. Is just frozen. But still moving the whole time, just a little, inside itself."

Linnæus replies: "Then glass is related to the mussels in the seas. After all, they are nothing but a fine moisture which has acquired a shell."

*

It is the 23rd of May. Linnæus's birthday. Now, if you must be Linnæus, you are to be Linnæus. But Linnæus feels fear.

What is Linnæus afraid of?

That he will find, when he goes out into his garden, that there is no garden.

That he will find, when he goes to look at his collections in their glass cases, that there are no glass cases and no collections there.

Of this he is afraid.

That the twenty-eight disciples will disappear. That his brothers and sisters will disappear.

He goes out into his garden every day, with a view to holding on to it. On these occasions he supplies himself with a motive. It can be a simple one. Like watering a particular plant with the green watering can. Removing some shoots on a shrub to prevent a too vigorous growth. Keeping couch-grass at bay.

This process is profane rather than sacred. Unlike some of the disciples and certain visitors, Linnæus does not apprehend the daily round in the garden as something close to an act of creation. More like an act of management. Or perhaps it is more correct to say that the creation, from the time that God left it, has in all probability taken the form of something to be managed, with, sometimes, human assistance.

Therefore he does not stop going out into the garden to give it his attention. He thinks that if he does not go out into the garden it will wither away and disappear.

*

The gardener shows Linnæus a leaf from a maple tree. On it are a number of black spots of varying shapes with yellow edges. The gardener knows that it is a parasitical fungus which attacks maple leaves. He holds the leaf close to his ear and listens: "Fungi are funny things," he says. "You do not know what they are doing. You do not know if they are animals or plants. You do not know anything."

"Rhytisma acerinum," Linnæus says, after a while.

*

It is the 23rd of July. The dog-days are here. Linnæus is standing in the garden, sweaty, dazed by the heat, and thinking about the stone fence he has decided to erect. Out there, in the fields, are the goats which come into his garden at night, laying it to waste and fouling it. He finds it strange that, according to the regulations, it is the owner of an estate who is responsible for fences. Surely it is the beasts' owners who should be fenced in, not the estates'.

The gardener: "At Lövsta the goats clamber right up onto the stone wall. They are made for the mountains. On Bielke's grounds the stone wall is the wildest, steepest thing there is. The goats want to be there and their wandering to and fro makes the stones loose."

*

October now. Linnæus summons the gardener.

"I have taken on Nietzel. He will be the chief gardener. You will be his assistant."

"Excellent," says the gardener.

"Dietrich Nietzel. George Clifford's head gardener at Hartekamp."

"Excellent," says the gardener.

"He has three thousand species under cultivation there. He will be bringing about three hundred plants with him. The boxes are being delivered and we can expect them here three days from now."

"Excellent," says the gardener.

*

It is night. Linnæus, unable to sleep, has gone out into the fields. He looks straight up at the sky. Stars are there, but no pictures. He presses his chin down onto his chest, bends his back, bends his knees, collapses, turns over, and comes up again. It was a somersault, and Linnæus feels heroic, and wretched.

*

The gardener takes Linnæus to a place a long way from the garden and shows him some plants. Linnæus recognizes them. They are *Alopecurus nigricans*, the meadow foxtail, which loves the salt of the sea.

But the gardener and Linnæus are on flat meadowland, far from the sea.

"It is the saltwater spring rising," says the gardener.

Linnæus wets a finger and tastes.

"Here, underneath us," says the gardener, "is the bottom of the Baltic."

*

Night. A figure is down among the paths. Linnæus looks down from his window. A man is leaning backwards and gazing up at him. Spitting. It is Rolander. His nosebleed.

Linnæus goes down, calls his name. Rolander clears his throat, spits, wipes his nostrils with his fists, rubs them against his coat, excuses himself, and pleads that he comes with greetings.

Linnæus carefully takes his time, pronounces different names, enquires after their health. Rolander replies:

"Sparschuch? Fell downstairs, dead. Wetterman? Burnt to death. Grufberg? Cut his throat with a razor, dead. Baeckner? Died of fever in Paris. Lutteman? Still living, insane. The Ferber brothers? Both died in poverty in America. Gisler? Mad, murdered three people. Edvall? Buried in Canton. Berzelius? Died on the way home from China. Lindh? Died on the ship *Terra Nova*. Lundberg? Died of fever in Stockholm. Carlbohm? Died of consumption in Paris. Björnståhl? Died of plague in Litocoro, Greece. Lundborg? Drowned. Salomon? Drowned. Luut? Drowned. Wennerdahl? Drowned. Söderberg? Drowned."

*

Linnæus calls out: "Gardener!"

There is something he wants to tell, to assert, exultantly. But the gardener looks worried, and it flags. The gardener shows Linnæus the palm of his hand. In it are a number of black spots of varying shapes, with yellow edges.

"I feel nothing," he says.

Linnæus sees how the spots are creeping inside the cuff of the gardener's shirt.

"Nothing," says Linnæus.

It is meant as a question, a question in response, but he can hear that it does not sound like a question.

"I do not feel like raking any more just now," says the gardener. "Not raking. Not just now."

✡

July. Slowly, very slowly, Dietrich Nietzel is moving northwards through Sweden. Through the ruins of old Axevall's castle, past stones bearing the inscriptions of the Swedish Goths, over Bråvalla heath, past Hallestrom's waterfall.

Out of the darkness a process of clarification is being prepared; a shift waiting to happen. From inn to inn he travels, asking the learned in each place about Linnæus and his garden.

✡

Linnæus is afflicted with palpitations and fainting fits. Tip of the nose cold. Sweats. Racing pulse.

✡

Wind. Suddenly October. Linnæus braces himself to go outside, led by the old assistant gardener, Lövberg. Linnæus is wearing his nightshirt and the red velvet skullcap.

They stand in the grove by the oak, the elm, and the ash to listen to the jingling of the hanging Aeolian bells of green glass. But no sound is heard. They think the jingling is being drowned out by the whistling of the wind and go right up to them. They sense the swaying of the leaves, each and every one of them. But from the glass bells they can distinguish only a muffled sound, dry and short, quite dull, like wood against felt.

Lövberg unhooks one of the bells and holds it to the light. It was formerly clear and completely transparent, but is now hazy, smudgy, watered. Linnæus, when he looks very carefully, can make out within the material fine grey threads stretching round the whole surface.

"The glass has stopped," Lövberg says. "It is the glass disease."

He moistens one of his fingertips and rubs the rim of the glass. There is no sound. He flicks a finger off the side.

"They will not be saying any more. They have stopped."

✡

The 28th of January. It is Carl's name day. Lövberg holds his hands and feels the coldness of his fingertips.

Give me a drink, Linnæus wants to say. But says: "To Ti! To Ti!"

Yet Lövberg understands. Linnæus has his own words in place of the usual ones. All the usual ones he has forgotten, one after the other. Thrown them high up. First, the nouns. *Monandria* and *Tetradynamia,* gone. Buttons, buttonholes, waistcoats, gone. Weasel, fish, knife, cheese — gone.

Lövberg mentions some well-known people's names.

Linnæus nods, then says, clearly and lucidly: "Yes."

But when he has to repeat the names, he is unable to, and instead writes on Lövberg's slip of paper: "Can nothing."

Lövberg names Odelius, Grisell, Kyronius. Linnæus nods. Lövberg writes the names on a slip of paper. Linnæus points to the names, nods, writes: "Can nothing."

When Lövberg strikes up the first verse of some psalm, it sometimes appears that Linnæus can sing it. He does not keep in tune, but he sings the verses distinctly and fluently.

Now and then he also pronounces certain prayers in time, as it were, in an exalted and clamorous voice.

But now Linnæus is saying nothing but: "To Ti! To Ti!"

Lövberg gives Linnæus a drink of water.

*

The 13th of April. Maundy Thursday. Report to George Clifford at Hartekamp, signed by Dietrich Nietzel, Hammarby, Sweden.

"All his limbs and organs, particularly his tongue, the lower extremities, and the bladder, are paralysed. His speech is rambling and unintelligible. Without help he cannot move from the place where he is sitting or lying, he cannot undress, eat, or perform the least of his needs. Of his organic life only the breathing, the digestion, and the circulation of the blood are still in reasonably good order. Everything else is more or less destroyed. He seems to be totally unaware of both past and present. There are only a few farmhands here. Garden in the worst state imaginable. Goats wandering about loose. My work is going to require great exertions and is already begun."

Translated from the Swedish by Harry D. Watson

MAGNUS FLORIN, born in 1955, is a dramaturge at the Royal Dramatic Theatre in Stockholm, and a writer. "The Garden" is an excerpt from a book of the same title (Stockholm, 1995).

Six Poems from a Work in Progress

SUSAN HOWE

Trench letters do get used
eventually for poetry you
long history of nihilism
Get ready to advance don't
everyone rattle camouflage
as if we are nothing only
company dive-bomb anxiety
A few persistent "islands"
of half inaudible whispers
jabbing the radioman Lethe

Photographs are very like
crossing the no-sail zone
Periscopes screens filters
no unused boots with me I
come home my dear mother he
wrote such harks each amok
embrasure an outlook bunker
I can face the world-facts
go burrowing after statistics
Realism all that fantasia

The hark of his attention
has no battle-dreams now
nor severe astasia-abasia
nor possible peace negotiation
nor newsreel shots crossing
to our civilian situation
nerves are in perfect order
Sea-drift the cry ice-floe
he is out with his wiring-party
Meantime incendiary weapons

Among the level down
go crash men flitting
Where are you whine shells
Scatter I see sentries
Up to the neck in war
O patiently people being
blown to bits one hand
clutching bandages next
bit *Proverbs* and byword
Language of escalation
this pun assembles down

Nominated as President by
dream-consciousness a cup
and saucer dream in three
collated lectures signed
by Amundsen saying he did
reach the Pole an aftermath
of fatigue postwar period
from its own wreck spoils
Before in the Dardanelles
taking off Sam Browne belt
Might solve sleeplessness
thus in my own Presidency

To be brief Kant's theory of
long run wars to hysteria
shock and projectile cycle
viz mimetic character until
a day is filled with night
night with doubt with doubt
Tense armies immemorial soil
reverberation of artillery
I equate will and instinct
with the other plot Europe
Cold marches with soldiers
abreast you cold Predicate

SUSAN HOWE's most recent book of poems is *The Nonconformist's Memorial* (New Directions, 1993). Her next book, *Frame Structures: Early Poems 1974–1979*, is forthcoming in the spring of 1996.

Juan Goytisolo and the Honor of the Novel

CARLOS FUENTES

1. THE VIRTUES OF THE SOLITARY BIRD

In a timely, perceptive article published in El País, José María Guelbenzu dissected the pallid fashion of "light" or "entertaining" literature, reminding us that literary creation is elitist; it is access to it that should be democratic, and "this is achieved only ... through a universal education that allows for the eradication of ignorance." When this occurs, Sterne, Stendhal, or Juan Goytisolo become accessible.

Guelbenzu also reminds us that democracy is not an act of laziness, mediocrity, or ignorance, but precisely this kind of demanding effort at education and lucidity, comparable, in a sense, to literary creation itself. Identifying literature with light entertainment in the name of popular accessibility does no service to either creation or democracy. In the long run, damaging the first means undermining the other.

In Spanish America people sometimes claim that works such as Lezama Lima's *Paradiso* or Julio Cortázar's *Rayuela* cannot be accepted by an uneducated, semiliterate public. My response has always been this: What will our illiterate people read when they do become literate, *Superman* or *Don Quixote*? The hope of a Lezama or a Cortázar in Latin America is the same as Guelbenzu's in Spain. "Novels must be entertaining," is the fashionable mandate. And Guelbenzu asks himself: "Isn't it just the reverse? Isn't it the reader who has to learn how to be entertained?"

At the center of this dispute stand readers and two different ways of inviting them to participate in the work of literature. One is the path of the best seller, which assumes an identifiable reader whose tastes, opinions, and prejudices are known ahead of time by the author, who then follows the recipe and puts together an attractive commercial dish. Readers don't read: they consume and perhaps are entertained, but the work passes through their intestines and emerges from what Juan Goytisolo calls "the steep precipice of the rectum."

The other way is to search out the reader who does not yet exist, the reader who remains to be created and discovered in the very act of reading. When this reader and the work meet, the potential novel is born. Its permanent residence is the shared mind and heart of Sterne and his reader, of Stendhal, Kafka, Joyce, and their readers. The reader and the work create each other.

Cortázar made a distinction, one that is perhaps too sexist for the late twentieth century, between the Male Reader (active) and the Female Reader (passive). I prefer to differentiate between the Meat Readers (male or female), who have to chew their food twenty times before swallowing it, and the toothless Gerber Readers (boys or girls), who down a bland, shapeless, pre-chewed pap.

The *apologia* for Gerber Readers takes many forms; they suck on many pacifiers and wear many bibs. If their lowest level is precisely this frivolous demand for "diverting" or "light" literature, the most mediocre is a realism that demands the subjugation of the verbal imagination to sociological statistics, psychological verisimilitude, and history conceived of as recordable fact but never as imagined time — present, past, or future.

In Mexico and Spanish America, the mediocrity of this demand is connected with a certain nostalgia for the identifiable, prosperous, democratic middle class we did not have at the height of realism during the last century. The critical anachronism of realism and psychologism, decked out in pretensions of historical objectivity, is equivalent to our current nostalgia for the mediating middle class, which, because it is in the middle, is virtuous and proudly mediocre. According to the realist anachronism, this would be the datum that reveals our "universality," for mediating mediocrity is where we prove that we are not different, that we are identical, for example, to the French and the English. We consume, in short, the same thing they, the "others," do, and this is how they, mediating and mediocre, become "us."

But the fact is that our universality, as a concrete datum of our humanity, does not recognize itself in this mediation of mediocrity. The great literature of Latin America consists of enormous leaps, supreme syntheses, violations of realism and its laws through the use of hyperbole, delirium, and dream. It is the creation of another history, a second history that blinds and diminishes archival historians. This second history is manifested in the writing of individuals, but proposes to be the memory and aspiration (in other words, the true reality) of a community that is, by definition, hurt. In the light of redemption, Adorno wrote, the world inevitably appears damaged.

This reality, which is an unreality in the eyes of naturalist *verismo* and calendar-based historicism, is the one that allows us, in Spanish America, to merge with a universality that is merely the sum of ancient eccentricities suddenly revealed as the centers of modern culture. This displacement transports us to the West Indies of Derek Walcott and V. S. Naipaul, the East Indies of Salman Rushdie, the Near West of Joan Didion and Norman Mailer, the insular eccentricity of Julian Barnes and Peter Ackroyd in England, the black Africa of Ben Okri, the Far South of Nadine Gordimer, and the Central European exile of Milan Kundera. All of this is the territory of the potential novel.

Realism, on the other hand, incapable of making the noncontemporary contemporary, condemns us to be anachronistic in the name of a so-called "truth." Making the past present is the hallmark of the art. It is denied by the notion of history as statistical, recordable fact rather than continual, imaginable event. The mainstay of this anachronism is usually the chauvinism that engages in the fascistic exclusion of those who, because of their lack of realism, do not deserve to be Mexicans, Spaniards, or Soviets.

The most literary defense of Gerber Readers is the one that demands a certain set of rules in order for the work to be accepted, a code based on a linear narrative with a logical beginning and end, psychologically rounded characters, and adherence to historic and social verisimilitude. This nineteenth-century realism did bear fruit— the greatest was Tolstoy — but it is a narrow exception to the literature that violates those same rules, from Rabelais, Cervantes, Sterne, and Diderot to Joyce, Faulkner, Virginia Woolf, and Broch, not to mention those "realistic" authors who, like Balzac, possess a totally fantastic dimension or, like Flaubert, are less interesting for their psychological *verismo* than for their style.

In our time, these positions still present themselves as opposites. I will cite two of their outstanding proponents. *Aspects of the Novel,* published in 1927 by E. M. Forster, codifies the laws of modern realism — aseptic, reductivist rules in which *Tristam Shandy* could be criticized as "obscure nonsense" at exactly the same time that themagazine Saturday Review offered an identical characterization of *The Castle* ("muddle" is what Forster called Sterne's work in 1927; in the same year, "rigamarole" was the term used by the New York magazine to describe Kafka's). What are they saying today, against this backdrop, about Goytisolo's *The Virtues of the Solitary Bird,* about Julian Rios's *Larva,* about all the books that don't fit into the narrow confines of a code incapable of reading them? They aren't saying anything, because reducing the work to something it is not, something it does not wish to be, is its negation.

The other position is best exemplified by Mikhail Bakhtin. The great Russian critic broadens the canon to include, within his concept of the dialogic novel (or polyphonic novel, as Broch would call it), a multiplicity of dialogues, not just between psychological "characters" within a "realistic" framework, but also between contradictory languages, distant historical periods, different social classes, or opposing historical visions which otherwise would not have the opportunity to engage in dialogue, to know one another through the imagination, which is how one *knows* in literature.

Bakhtin's creative freedom suits the contemporary novel, allows for its potentiality conceived of in verbal terms, but also, through the use of language, in dynamic, active terms that are historical, political, and even national; meat, not pap; inclusivity, not exclusivity. This is the honor of the contemporary novel, peerlessly embodied and defined by Juan Goytisolo.

His novel *The Virtues of the Solitary Bird* has been the target of criticism that reflects either the longing for "entertaining," "light" facileness, or adherence to the proven rules that Goytisolo radically demolishes. Too much smoke and no fire, as the critics have said? On the contrary: the smoke is equivalent to the hellfire that produced it, but it also lets fly with a few purgatories, and its verbal barrage forces open the gates of a forbidden paradise — the heaven where entities meet through the texts that write them and allow them to touch when all the world's laws forbid their meeting.

Goytisolo's *Solitary Bird* brings together all the aspects of the text that Bahktin desires and Forster rejects. It should be judged by its fidelity to the laws that affirm it, not the ones that ignore it. It is not a dialogue between psychological characters, it is not a linear narration, it has no visible plot, it does not have a clear beginning and end. Instead, its dialogue takes place among three texts: the work of Saint John of the Cross; the Sufi poetry, with its great mystic, ascetic, and quietist freight, of Ibn al-Farid, al-Ghazali, and Jalal al-Din Rumi; and Goytisolo's own contemporary text, a present-day possibility and impossibility of the previous ones. The narrative, in order to embrace this textual material, has to be sinuous and simultaneous. Like all great novels, it is a displacement. But at the same time, the journey is an elliptical argument that leads us from the "text that represents the quotidian" (the set of rules that is realistic, transparent, directly intelligible) to the radically unintelligible text, an "insoluble enigma" that takes on "the turns of phrase of its jagged, tense language."

Upon discovering, by means of Goytisolo's writing, the mystery in a text that seemed obvious because it was customary, readers are obliged to return to the text itself, see it with new eyes, undertake a second reading. Then they discover that they did not really read the first time because they were not puzzled. They thought (hoped) it was a text representing the quotidian, and upon rereading found instead an "insoluble enigma." But between clarity and mystery, a third displacement (a third journey, third reading, third plot) obliges readers to take the text literally: to really read it, not to accept it as a given or as an impenetrable mystery, but to see, for the first time, what is really there.

And what is there is ambiguity, part transparency and part mystery. What is there is "burning ecstasy and utter suspension of the senses," "tyrannical movements of the body," "ardor, sweating, fainting," the "raptures, visions, and pleasures of perpetual chastity." As in Faulkner, as in Beckett, in Goytisolo the plot is not prescribed. It is found only by making the journey from the quotidian text to the enigmatic text to the ambiguous text, which is, in the end, the *literal* text in the truest sense of the word.

The plot is this: "... from the age of seven a beautiful young man began to meet her in secret and she was betrothed to him and lived with him in matrimony, a fact she revealed to no one since this was the Beloved."

A mystic plot having to do with one who cannot live without God. But also a physical plot of one who seeks the beloved, finds him in secret, inclines her face over him, surrenders, feels her throat wounded, tears the cloth of the sweet encounter, and lies sleeping with the beloved body. And, naturally, a dramatic plot, escaping on a dark night from the sleeping house by means of deceit, using disguises, protected by darkness: a drama of silence, shadow, and burning desire ...

Unamuno's "intrahistory" begins to be visible, but only because of a fact of the writing: the breakdown of the realistic system that promised "transparency" but gave "mystery" instead because it convinced us that what was legible only in the text was visible in reality. "A breakdown in the system of equivalences, an infinite expansion of the sense of words." This is the author's handiwork, and by means of it he infinitely enriches Saint John's text, the texts of the Sufi poets, and Juan Goytisolo's own text. Just as the Bride and the Beloved are joined, so the Text and the Text are made one. And just as the Bride is transformed into the Beloved, so the Text is transformed into an Other Text.

The beautiful, impassioned operation performed by Goytisolo on one of the supreme texts of our language is not only an homage; it is a necessity and has a triple purpose: historic, erotic, and moral.

Historically, it joins what time and prejudice have separated: the poetry of Saint John, its Persian antecedents, and our own modern language.

Erotically, it realizes the miracle of denying the discontinuity of beings by reuniting them through a literary text. This is nothing new: Don Quixote and Dulcinea, Romeo and Juliet, Cathy and Heathcliff transcend their separation only in the text — the conqueror of death and the sole triumph possible for eroticism.

And morally, *The Solitary Bird* is a transgressive, violating, heretical text. But its heresy is that of Pelagius against Saint Augustine: Grace requires no mediation other than the word and the one who pronounces it; it is accessible to all and does not depend on our submission to religious or political hierarchies. In the novel I detected a premonition worthy of Henry James. "The fact he mentions has not yet occurred," writes Goytisolo. Can this fact be an unexpected rebellion? And can this rebellion be a parallel revolutionary turn toward the sacred and the erotic, joined together in poetry? And are there any better presences for the undertaking than Saint John of the Cross, the Sufi poets, and the Spanish novelist?

The work of Juan Goytisolo represents an extraordinary contribution in Spanish to the permanent revolution in contemporary narrative. Pursued by anachronism, chauvinism, the ruins of realism, tunnel vision, "entertaining," "light" frivolity, rationalist terrorism, and psychic insecurity: the geography of the modern novel makes use of all these barriers in order to transcend them and broaden, in the face of all detractors, the horizon of human possibility in history. This is the living tradition of the novel. In the case of Juan Goytisolo, where does the tradition come from and toward what possibility is it heading?

2. LANDSCAPES AFTER THE BATTLE

Spanish culture, from Cervantes to Buñuel, has been created in countertime. While, generally speaking, the English and French traditions were made to the rhythm of modernity, the Spanish tradition was formed in opposition to whatever denied it. First the repressive edicts of the Catholic sovereigns, Isabel and Ferdinand, expelling the Jews and proclaiming purity of blood, and the Catholic religion, as the bases for national unity. Then a strict application in Spain of the norms of the Council of Trent that turned Spain into the fortress of the Counter-Reformation.

Writing against the current became an anguished yet comic habit for Fernando de Rojas, the author of *La Celestina* (1499), and for Mateo Alemán, author of *Guzmán de Alfarache* (1599). Rojas's tragicomedy inaugurates the novel of modernity — urban, transient, disillusioned, internalized. Its author eventually takes refuge in his profession as a country lawyer. *Guzmán* originates the picaresque tale of modern displacement in Europe. Mateo Alemán goes into exile in Mexico so that his fame will die. What does not die is a rebellious tradition that leads to the erotic magnificence of novels by Francisco Delicado (*La lozana andaluza*, 1528) and María de Zayas (*El Decameron español*, 1637).

Juan Goytisolo transforms these literary traditions into internalized readings of modernity. Thanks to Goytisolo, the tradition of the Spanish past becomes our present. Saint John of the Cross and Ibn Arabi, Zayas and Delicado, Rojas and Alemán, Quevedo and *Estebanillo González*: The broadest tradition, the one that embraces them all and allows them to be read in the most radical fashion, is, for Goytisolo and many others, the tradition of Cervantes.

Francisco Márquez Villanueva, one of Goytisolo's finest critics, states that Cervantesizing is a process parallel to Judaisizing and Islamisizing. *Don Quixote* sums up the traditions that range from the *Libro de buen amor* to *La Celestina* and foretells their continuation in Zayas and Delicado, establishing comic values that in and of themselves implied "a militant opposition to the oppressive rigidities of a dogmatic, inquisitorial society." Cervantes gathers up, includes, disguises everything prohibited by "the aesthetic precepts officially supported by the Church-State bloc." The process is not negative, however. Cervantes affirms a modernity in countertime that is obliged to imagine not only what the Counter-Reformation denies but even what the reformist modernity of the West has forgotten.

Countertime in two senses — contrary to the reactionary beat of Spain, contrary to the progressive beat of the West: Cervantes creates a critical, imaginative modernity that concedes to literature the privilege of creating reality, not merely reflecting it, through the multiplication of texts that depend on multiple readings, not merely on a single orthodox and racially pure reading.

Cervantine uncertainty in contrast to the certainty and orthodoxies of the Counter-Reformation: uncertain names (Quijote, Quijano, Quijotiz? Aldonza, Dulcinea?); uncertain authorship (Cervantes? Saavedra? Cide Hamete? Avellaneda?); uncertain narrator (I, You, He, We?); uncertain place (La Mancha, Oblivion?). Overlapping of genres: a rupture in the purity of a post-Tridentine world that demanded a single language and a single vision. A self-conscious novel that rejects the illusion of being a simple reflection of reality. A critical modern novel that earns the right to criticize the world because it first criticizes itself. And a novel of displacements and constant peril, in which no discovery is a refuge: Cervantes and Goytisolo, outdoor writers because their novels and their characters go out into the world, leave the village, take risks: they emigrate.

Goytisolo places these traditions in the service of the most radical theme of our modernity: the Other, the Immigrant, the Displaced Person, the bearer of mestizo cultures who challenges our prejudices, our ability to give and receive, the capacity of our intelligence to understand and be understood.

Goytisolo's great novel *Landscapes after the Battle*, published in 1982, prophesies the theme that would come to occupy the center of our attention as the twentieth century ends and the twenty-first begins. In 1989, Juan and I met in Berlin and visited the Wall. Juan insisted we see it from Kreuzberg, the district of Turkish immigrants, as if he could already foresee not only the toppling of one wall a few months later but also the immediate raising of another that bars admittance to the immigrant. Before anyone else, and in Spanish, in *Landscapes* Goytisolo discovered how to write the novel of the other, of the immigrant and his displacements. Far from any philanthropic or propagandistic intention, he endowed the event and its protagonists with a narrator and narrative material, a language and a space, thereby inaugurating the novel of the migrant city for the coming century, as Rojas invented the unwalled city-in-movement for Renaissance modernity.

"Africa begins on the boulevards," and the first theme of *Landscapes after the Battle* is displacement. Lukács has said that there is no novel without displacement. From Troy to Lolita, the novel is the privileged space (epic, dramatic, satiric) of physical displacement: Celestina moves within a new, dynamic city, followed by her court of Lazarillos, Buscones, and Justinas; Robinson travels to a desert island in the Pacific; Don Quixote leaves his village for the broad fields of Montiel. Jacques follows his master along the roads of France, David Copperfield emigrates from bucolic tranquillity to London's suffocating fog of brick and coal, Rastignac goes to Paris, Jules Verne to the center of the earth. Lermontov seeks death in the Caucasus, Dostoevsky in a yellow neighborhood of Petersburg. Vast spaces in Melville and Turgenev. Joseph de Maîstre's journey around a room. The plains of James Fenimore Cooper empty into the California of Raymond Chandler and Nathanael West. Poe travels to the heart of ice but also to the telltale heart of walled-in death, and Conrad, as we all know, journeys to the heart of darkness.

For displacement is also internal, and Freudian: the elaboration of dreams; omission, modification, substitution; a change in the object of desire; the erotic dream disguised, transformed into a social dream. Goytisolo's originality is that he merges the two displacements, the external and the internal, into a single contemporary diaspora. His place is the city. His protagonist is the immigrant. The resonance that Goytisolo brings to this subject is due, as we've said, to the breadth of the tradition it embraces — the Cervantine tradition, to locate it along its novelistic axis. But the axis of the tradition is mythic as well — in *The Quarantine,* his beautiful chronicle of an accompanied death, the writer is displaced in order to accompany his friend, his beloved, on the journey to death. Accompanied, in turn, by both the novelistic tradition and the ritual tradition of displacement, Goytisolo, contemporary author in the Spanish language, goes out to his encounter with the Other.

The encounter takes place thanks to the narrative language and not to sentimental good intentions. Technique and content are associated in *Landscapes after the Battle* because the authorial "I," which is the character's "I," is united (fused, joined) with the "narrator," who is the Author-plus-characters found throughout the text. Goytisolo achieves this polyphonic result through the crossing of pronouns, verbal tenses, and cultures. The mestizaje of form merges with the mestizaje of subject. I will cite one chapter of the book, "The Appointment," in which the narrative "I" becomes a "he" ("he tells him") verging on possessive plurality ("our unfortunate hero"). Finally, the narrated-narrator "no longer knows if it is the remote individual who usurps his name or that goytisolo who is creating him." What we know is that before our very eyes a "peripatetic subject of narration" has been established in which the character is multiple as well as the narrator, and in them voices foreign to both converge. At the same time, the narrators, the bearers of those voices, also converge to create a linguistic mestizaje corresponding to the racial and cultural mestizaje that is the theme of the novel.

In Goytisolo the antecedent is evident, and Hispanic: to mestizize is to Cervantesize, and to Cervantesize is to Islamisize and Judaisize; it is to embrace again the exiled and persecuted, to rediscover the vocation of inclusion, to transcend the curse of exclusion. It is to marginalize the centers and attack the margins in multiple centers. Goytisolo gives extraordinary force to the reinclusion of the excluded because he grafts it onto another great novelistic tradition, the one that puts an end to the linguistic unity that belonged to the classicil age or to the perverted nostalgia for classicism that defines periods of orthodoxy. In the classical world, everyone understands everyone else: Priam and Agamemnon, Paris and Achilles. But Don Quixote does not understand Sancho, and Sancho does not understand him. The members of the Shandy family do not understand one another. Madame Bovary does not understand her husband, and Anna Karenina does not understand hers. The novel must have recourse to humor in order to admit that there are many manners of speaking, that things can be said in many ways. The language of the novel, writes Shklovsky, is a continuing re-elaboration of all levels of language; language, as Cervantes, Balzac, Shaw, and Raymond Queneau all knew, is diverse because it is stratified, and stratified because its forms of speech belong to societies that are not only diversified but also separate and unjust. Now they are also foreign societies, Babels in which the immigrant appears as the bearer of yet another language that is often not even the common language of the nation. When Goytisolo, in his Sentier quarter in Paris, suddenly found himself surrounded by Turkish immigrants, he did what every human being possessing a modicum of humor, reason, and love should do: he learned to speak Turkish.

The linguistic impulse of the modern novel, its hybrid, parodic, imitative, derivative character, attempts to transcend the impurities of its origin with the oldest of sanitizing procedures: the "poeticization" that converts language into an image of language. A tenacious mestizaje looks for and finds new ways to sneak in, make its presence felt, infect, and parody the abstract language of Western sanitation and oblige it to show itself as cliché, as political rubble (and political wall), as commercial advertising. In this sense, with *Landscapes* Goytisolo brings to a culmination the thematic-verbal revolution begun by Flaubert with *Bouvard et Pécuchet*. Except that Goytisolo also returns to the Arcipreste de Hita, and in France to Rabelais, in order to attack linguistic unity and have us submit to the language of the other.

The arena for these encounters, as we know, is the city. The urban theme in narrative is as old as the Trojan horse and the escapades of Petronius. But the city as the seat of modernity is an invention of what Donald Fanger calls "the romantic realism" of Balzac, Dickens, and Dostoevsky. What Rastignac, Pip, or Roskolnikov discover is, once again and yet again, what Celestina and Guzmán de Alfarache already knew: the modern city, stripped of its walls and moats, is an open, transient place in which the values of the ancient city — honor, rank, courtliness — vanish, overrun by ambition, money, and sex. Gogol, in the brilliant opening of *The Nevsky Prospect*, imagines a wasted city in which we see nothing but shattered ruins. We would like to reconstruct unity so that we ourselves can be One. The romantic aspiration for unity regained is denied, only to be reaffirmed by the fragmented image of urban civilization in the twentieth century. Now the open city has been conquered from within, whether it is the Dublin of Joyce, the Petersburg of Biely, the Berlin of Döblin, or the Manhattan of Dos Passos. But this defeat of unity: couldn't it also be the triumph of diversity, of the "polytheism of values" alluded to by Max Weber?

Perhaps we have not known how to admit and profit from urban "polytheism." Today, a "sentimental education" means the teaching of mestizaje. Like it or not, the "polytheistic" city is already here. The energy of Hispanic cities in the United States, such as Miami or Los Angeles, in fact depends on their mestizo character. Los Angeles, which is not only Hispanic but Korean, Vietnamese, Chinese, and Japanese, promises to become the Byzantium of the twenty-first century. A great novelty for Latin Americans: for the first time, we are beginning to resemble North Americans. What makes us similar is the shared crisis of our urban civilizations: Los Angeles and Mexico City, Detroit and Rio, New York and Caracas, Lima and Atlanta...

Goytisolo does not evade the theme of the city ruined from within. He even calls it "the city of the dead": "... you can find the future metropolis here: ruins vestiges rubble of a prosperous civilization that has been razed..." The apocalyptic vision has its laughable side. In *Landscapes after the Battle* comic accidents abound, incidents worthy of the mistreated heroes of modern urban civilization — Buster Keaton, Woody Allen, Peter Sellers. The urban comic hero detests the odor of vinegar; in the crowded movie, he sits right next to the man who smells of vinegar. His lack of manual dexterity is absolute; he doesn't know how to change a tire or cut a steak correctly. He goes out and reads only contemptible headlines: Julio Iglesias and Margaret Thatcher are having a secret affair. He goes to a political meeting at the Opera in Paris, and they play "Clavelitos," the folk tune he most despises.

The somber side, however, brings a desire for victory. The cities are already at war, they are the battleground: "The district has been cordoned off." Objective war, as demonstrated by events in Rio de Janeiro and Los Angeles during the quincentenary year. And individual, subjective war, masterfully evoked in *Quarantine*. In short, a war of collective individuality, which is to say of culture and those who remember it, create it, and prolong it: all of us. In this world, God is merely a "voice off" commenting on the perpetual crisis of modernity while the novelist endlessly composes and recomposes it, writing outdoors, refusing any shelter except the embrace of the newcomer, the bearer of the other face, the other skin, the other cuisine, the other faith, the other language. Dostoevsky called cities an "accidental tribe." No description has ever been more exact. In the city, with the other, according to how we accept or reject him, the possible civilization of the next century will be created. But the signs are ominous. Xenophobia, racism, anti-Semitism, anti-Islamism, rejection of the South American in Spain, the Turk in Germany, the Arab in France; a resurgence of Nazism: Will the death of Communism authorize the resurrection of Fascism?

I have formulated a question. In *Quarantine*, Goytisolo affirms nothing; the entire text is a question, many questions. As she was dying, Gertrude Stein asked Alice B. Toklas, "What's the answer?" Toklas did not respond. Stein understood her and said, "Then what's the question?" before she turned her back (on Alice, on the world) and died. Goytisolo's question assumes the risk not of an answer, but of a fraternal act surrounded by abysses: Is there another voice; isn't it also mine? Is there another skin, another faith, another history, another dream; aren't they mine too? Goytisolo discovers that all worlds are both new and old, and dangerously open. His prose is the disease and the cure: an epidemic of contacts, alienations, and communions. We know the world; now we must imagine it.

Translated from the Spanish by Edith Grossman

CARLOS FUENTES, Mexico's leading novelist, was born in 1928. He has written many essays and screenplays, collaborated with Luis Buñuel, and been his country's ambassador to France. In November 1987, he was awarded the Cervantes Prize. His novels include *Where the Air Is Clear*, *The Old Gringo*, *Terra Nostra* and *A Change of Skin*. EDITH GROSSMAN is a critic and translator of contemporary Latin American literature. Her most recent translations include *Of Love and Other Demons*, by Gabriel García Márquez, *The Adventures of Maqroll*, by Alvaro Mutis, *Complete Works and Other Stories*, by Augusto Monterroso, and *Death in the Andes*, by Mario Vargas Llosa.

SIX POEMS

PIA TAFDRUP

Caravan

To my sister

Icy fields, snow-covered woods
frost that burns into the skin
No paths to follow only planes we cross alone
and long after each other
It's scarcely us moving our feet
rather the earth carrying us forward

We are living —
which means:
We are fighting death
in all its embodiments
Everything we say will be used against us
but so will everything we don't

Icy fields, snow-covered woods
a sky growing dense
dark as a wailing wall
The snow-laden sky, a Jewish graveyard
kilometers of white stones sprung up
among the spruces in the forests outside Kiev

With every flake I focus on
I slowly dream that I am here:
Spirit in blood in snow in the world
Inward —
to blaze recklessly
and then be gone in the whiteness.

Horizon

Like proffered grains of salt
Jerusalem springs up
from the mountains

Red and pink limestone
a desert all around
that obeys and blossoms

Time
is momentary
and millennial

Aeolian harps
migrating sand
evening sun

Voices
brush the ear
which scans the pain:

In the dark under the fishing-tackle hatch
my father and his family in a cutter
across the Sound to Sweden

In the bottom of another boat my mother's father
and on a shelf in the engine room
my mother and her mother . . .

Count the multitude
see each one
no limit must be set, no one forgotten

The mound of each consciousness
a memory
that keeps dread awake

The day is large
as a hefting-stone
I bend toward the silent paper

spin a life's thread.

The Mount of Olives

The entrance to life is the same for all,
and the exit from it is also the same.
— *Wisdom of Solomon 7:6*

Calm in the sun, the graveyard on the Mount of Olives
where caravans of stone head off across the western slopes
Calm as those landscapes that suddenly switch to desert
places that have still not been given names
where sand blows and settles in ever new formations
Calm the air, a rent in your garment
and night on the mountain soft as under a bird's wing
Calm is the air between the graves
on which stones bloom eternally for the dead
— Praised be the Judge of truth —
Calm as in Jerusalem's depths, where water drips
in cisterns over two millennia old
echoes of souls that still hold vigil
Each drop falls with its *platt,*
one syllable, like the word dead.

Infection

You stiffen, poisoned by sudden dread
while the day founders and changes color
and the blood behind a steadily rising pulse
spreads pain into the finest vessels
where it flutters around like ash
that a wingbeat lifts above the embers
until the heart — that coral tree
acutely blossoming — stands still in a cramp,
on the point of drowning in its own blood
For who can go on his way immune
in a city where people live separated
like shards of the same dream
The darkness piercing a stranger
— will the hatred invade you?
Like shrapnel that gnaws into your flesh
far, far from that morning when, new-born,
you were blessed by the first light.

A Thousand Times Recalled

Green here too, where since early summer the soil's crust
has resembled the furrowed skin that hangs from the cheekbones of aged women;
where the houses carry scars and memory's images fall, as dense as raining bullets
The eucalyptus trees on the hillside do not remember yesterday
just as the sparrows do not long for tomorrow

Horned cattle and flocks of sheep, spread across Jerusalem's plains;
flowers poised to spring out, and people who dance up the slopes
to pick them too early, reaching deep into silence so the yellow butterflies
are shaken loose and sail up into the air
in a radiance of signs, a gentle metallic swaying:

One of many or each single one — that makes all the difference
when refugees are hidden in the bottom of fishing boats
on their way to another country
with each their prayer for the same thing
To be lifted across the water.

Exit

From the mountain to the north you can see the birds from above
floating away across the valley
Their shadows, which glide by like a lifetime,
make space expand with a quiver
their cries resonate between sheer cliffs
Syncopated they climb, sail away lovesick in the thin air
vanish at the horizon, no different from wisps of cloud
The stillness here has wings, so the far-off spring
sounds close up, like an apocryphal murmur
My gaze follows each movement with an unquenchable thirst
even before it occurs
Not a colorless landscape, a dust-white haze
but colors that comprise all color
have dried into my mind
where any rash thought
would leap like a spark
and could easily ignite the withered grass
that even early in the year is dizzily fragrant of hay
Only the valley floor is green
an interior ocean exalted by calm:
as soon as we had left Jerusalem, we found we were on our way back.

Translated from the Danish by Roger Greenwald

PIA TAFDRUP, Danish poet, is a member of the Royal Danish Academy. The poems published here will be included in a forthcoming collection of poetry. ROGER GREENWALD, American poet and translator, lives in Toronto and edits the literary annual writ.

Letter to the Amazon

MARINA TSVETAEVA

I read Your book. You are close to me as are all women who write. Don't be offended by that "all" — all do not write and only few of all women do.

So, You are close to me as each unique being is, and, especially, as each unique female being is.

I've been thinking of You since the day I first saw You — a month ago? When I was young, I was in a rush to express myself, I was always afraid to let the wave cresting in me and carrying me to another go, I was afraid that I would fall in love no more: that I would learn nothing more. But I'm not young anymore and I've learned to let almost everything go — beyond recall.

To have everything to say — yet clench your lips. Everything to give — and clench your palm. That's the renunciation which You call bourgeois virtue and which, bourgeois or not, virtue or not — is the driving force of my actions. Renunciation? Force? Yes, because suppression of energy demands an infinitely greater effort than its free release — which demands no effort at all. In that sense all natural activity is passive, in the same way that passivity is active (release — submission, suppression — action).

What's harder: to restrain a horse or let it gallop? And, since the horse we restrain is we ourselves, what's more torturous: to be held back or to give our force free rein? To breathe or not? Do You remember that children's game, where the winner is the child who can stay longest in a stuffy trunk, *without suffocating*? A cruel and hardly bourgeois game.

To act? To let oneself go? Each time I renounce, I sense the earth's tremor inside me. Trembling earth: I am she. What is renunciation? Petrified struggle.

My renunciation has yet another name: don't descend to the existing order. The existing order in our case? To read Your book, to thank You for it with empty words, to see You again from time to time "smiling, to conceal Your smile," to pretend that You'd written nothing and I, read nothing: as if nothing had happened.

I could have done that, I still can now, but this time around I don't want to.

Please listen. You don't have to answer. You must only hear me out. I aim straight to the heart — to the core of Your care, Your flesh, Your faith, Your heart.

There is a gap in Your book, just one, but enormous. Is it conscious or not? I don't believe in the unconscious of thinking beings, still less of thinking and writing beings, and I don't believe at all in the unconscious of women writing.

This gap, this gape, this black cleft is the Child.

You constantly return to it, You mention it frequently, but You deny its importance. You scatter it here, there, and over there, depriving it of the integrity of the single cry You owe it.

That cry — can it be that You've never even at least heard it: "If only I could have a child by you!"

And that jealousy, savage and singular in its kind, implacable because incurable, incomparable to any "normal" jealousy, even a mother's? That jealousy, prescience of inevitable rupture, those eyes gaping wide toward the child that she will one day desire, and that You, the elder one, won't be able to give her. Those eyes riveted on the future child.

"Lovers have no children."Yes, but they die. All. Romeo and Juliet, Tristan and Isolde, the Amazon and Achilles, Siegfried and Brünnhilde (these omnipotent lovers united by separation, whose amorous separation surpasses even the most perfect union ...). And the others ... And still others ... From all songs, all times and all lands ... They lack time for a future, which is the child. They lack a child, for they have no future. All they've got is the present — their ever-present love and death. They die — or their love dies (reduced to friendship or to mothering: old Baucis and her old Philemon, or old Pulcheria and her old man-child Afanasy — couples as monstrous as they are touching).

Love by itself is childhood. Lovers are children. Children never beget children.

Or, like Daphnis and Chloe, we learn nothing more of them: even if they live on, they have died, in us, for us.

One cannot *live* by love. The single thing that outlives love: the Child.

And that other cry, can it be that You've never heard it, either? "How much I'd like a child — without a man!" Smiling sigh of a young girl, wistful sigh of an old maid, and on occasion even the hopeless sigh of any woman: "How much I'd like one — all *my very own!*"

And now this smiling young girl, craving in her body nothing alien, neither a him nor a his, wanting only *my very own*, encounters at a turning in the road another *I*: a *she,* whom she need not fear, from whom she need not defend herself, since this "other" cannot harm her, for one cannot (at least when young) harm oneself — a certitude most illusory, which will shudder at her lover's first mistrustful glance and collapse under the onslaught of her heartfelt hate.

But let's not run ahead: for the moment she is happy and free, free to love with her heart, without body, to love without fear, to love without harm.

But when the harm is done, she discovers that it's not harm at all. Harm is: shame, regret, remorse, revulsion. Harm is to betray her soul with a man, to betray her childhood to the enemy. Yet there is no enemy, for this is still *me,* always *me,* a new me, which was dormant in my depths, but now roused by this other *me,* there, before me, come to the surface, and, at last, *lovable.* She had no need to deny herself to become a woman; she had only to let herself go (to the very core of her being), only let herself be. No wound, no rupture, no dishonor.

And this word, saying it all:

"Oh me, *my* beloved!"

She won't ever leave her for shame or revulsion. But for another (an other) reason.

At the outset it is nothing more than an idle joke.

"What a lovely baby!"

"Wouldn't you like one?"

"Yes. No. By you — yes."

But . . . but it's all in jest.

The next time it's already a sigh.

"How much I'd like a . . ."

"Yes, what?"

"Oh, nothing."

"No, no, I know . . ."

"Well, if you already know. But only — by you."

Silence.

"Are you still thinking about that?"

"If you say so."

"But you're the one who keeps saying . . ."

She lacks nothing, but she has too much — *everything* in her — yet to give. "I wish I could love a little you." The same way a woman says (to a man): "I wish I could love a little you. Another you. Boy or girl. One more you. Made child by me."

And at last, a cry, desperate, naked, and undeniable: "A child by you!"

The one who will never come. The one whose coming one can't even pray for. One can plead with Mary for a child by a lover, one can plead with Mary for a child by an old man — beyond justice, a miracle even — but one can't ask for madness. A union from which the child is simply excluded. Presupposing the absence (unthinkability) of the child. Everything, but the child. Like that supper of the Great King and the nobleman: everything but bread. Great bread, daily bread: woman.

Child: ever the desperate desire of one of them, the younger one, the more *she*. The older one needs no child, she has her friend to mother: "You are my darling, my god, my all."

But the younger one doesn't want *to be loved* like a child; she wants a child *to love*.

She who began by not wanting a child by *him* will end by craving a child by *her*. And because that cannot be, one day she will go away, *continuing to love*, but driven by the clear and impotent jealousy of the other — and she will one day run aground, shipwrecked, into the arms of the first man who comes along.

(My child, my darling, my all, and — as You brilliantly say, Madame — my girl-brother: my never-sister. Presumably the word "sister" scares them, as though it's capable of returning them by force to a place they left forever.)

At the outset the older one fears it more than the other desires it. One could say it's the older one who drives her to despair, turning smile into sigh, sigh into desire, desire into obsession. The obsession of the younger one is born in the obsession of the older: "You will leave, you will leave, you will leave. You want a child by me, you'll want it of the first man who comes along... You're still thinking about it... You looked at that man. A fine father for your child, don't you think! Leave me, since I can't give it to you..."

Our apprehensions propose, our fears — intimate, our obsessions — body forth. The younger one, forced to keep silent, thinks of it constantly; she can't keep her eyes from young women with their arms filled. "Just think: I will never have one, because I never, never will leave her." (And at this moment she leaves her.) The child — a fixed point from which she can't tear her eyes. The child submerged in her comes again to the surface of her eyes like a drowned person. You'd have to be blind not to see it there.

And she who began by craving a child by *her* will end by craving a child no matter by whom: even by him, the hated one. Her predator becomes her savior. The beloved — the enemy. And the wind returns again according to its circuits...

The child is conceived in us long before its conception. There are pregnancies that take years of hope, eternities of despair.

And all the girlfriends around her keep getting married. The husbands of her friends, so cheerful, so gregarious, so comprehensible... "Come to think of it: I, too..."

Immured.

Buried alive.

And the older one can't let go. Hints, reproaches, suspicions. The younger one: "Don't you love me anymore?" "I love you, but all the same you will go."

You will go, you will go, you will go.

Prior to going, she'll want to die. And so, heavy with death, unconscious of anything, unwittingly, unintentionally, by a pure and triply vital instinct — youth, time, loins — she'll hear herself, at the time of the never-missed rendezvous, laughing and joking at the other end of town — and of life — with whomever — with one of her friends' husbands or her father's employees, so long as it's not *she*.

Man, after woman — what simplicity, what generosity, what frankness. What liberty! What purity.

Then will be the end. The first lover? A stream of them? The stable husband?

Then will be the Child.

I omit the exceptional case: the woman without maternal instinct.

I omit also the banal case: the girl, corrupted by her own sensuality or by fashion: existing for pleasure only and not warranting attention.

I omit as well the rare case: the forsaken soul, one that even in love quests for soul — predestined for a woman.

And love's glutton, who seeks in love love alone and takes its measure wherever she finds it.

And the clinical case.

I'm dealing with the normal case, the usual human affair: a young female creature, fearful of a man, gets drawn to a woman, but craves a Child. Finding herself between him — alien to her, indifferent, even an enemy, but *able to reveal her essence* — and the beloved, *able to repress it,* she ends by choosing the enemy.

She who craves having a child more than loving.
She who loves her child more than her own love.

For the Child is something innate, present in us even prior to love, prior to the beloved. It's his desire to exist that makes us throw our arms wide. A young girl — I'm speaking of those from the north — is always too young for love, but never for the child. At thirteen she already dreams of it.

Something innate that must be given to us. Some start with love for the one who gives it, others end with love for him, still others end by submitting to him, and others end by submitting to him no more.

Something innate, that we should be given. Whoever does not give it takes it away.

And so we find her again, with arms filled and with heartfelt hatred toward her whom she will henceforth dub — ungrateful, like all who don't love anymore, and unjust, like all who keep on loving — a "youthful indiscretion."

By this she won't be seduced again.

Don't get cross with me. I reply to the Amazon and not to some white feminine specter that asks nothing of me. Not to the one who gave me the book, but the one who wrote it.

If You hadn't mentioned the child at all, I would have taken that for a conscious omission, the ultimate renunciation, through silence, a scar I would have respected. But You return to it constantly, You bounce it around like a ball: "By what right do women create and destroy life? Two offspring — two oversights," etc.

It is the single flaw, the single weak point, the single crack in that splendid whole that two women loving each other constitute. Unlike desire for a man, the craving for a child one can't resist.

The single flaw because of which everything crumbles. The single weak point, through which the whole enemy force penetrates. For even if we could one day have a child *without him,* we will never be able to have a child by her — a little you to love.

(An adopted daughter? Neither mine nor yours? With, furthermore, two mothers? No, better let nature run its course.)

The child: the single weak point because of which the entire kind collapses. And what saves that of man — and mankind, too.

Entirety too entire. Unity too one. ("Two will become but one." No — two will become *three.*) The road that leads nowhere. A cul-de-sac. Let's turn back.

"And no matter how gorgeous you might be, no matter how unique, the first available nobody will make a conquest of you. The nobody will be blessed. And you will remain cursed."

"But it's precisely the same when one cannot have a child by *this* man. Is that a reason to abandon him?"

The exceptional case can't be compared to a rule without exception. For in every case of love between women, the entire tribe, the entire kind, the entire thing is condemned.

To abandon an infertile man for his fertile brother is nothing like abandoning the eternally infertile *her* for an eternally fertile enemy. There I bid farewell to but one man, here it's the entire tribe, to the entire kind, to all women in one.

To change only the object. To change the shore and the world.

Oh, I know, sometimes this sort of thing lasts till the very death. A touching and terrifying vision: a wild Crimean shore, two women, already aged, who have spent their entire life together. One of them was the sister of the great Slavic thinker so much read now in France. The same clear brow, the same raging gaze, the same fleshy, naked lips. But they are surrounded by more emptiness than surrounds a "normal" aged and childless couple — a more estranging, more devastating emptiness.

For nothing, nothing more than that — cursed race.

It is, perhaps, the horror of this curse that compels her, provided she is astute, to abandon the other.

"What will people say?" means nothing and must mean nothing, for no matter what people say, they will say foul, and, no matter what they see, they will see foul. Evil eye of envy, curiosity, indifference. There's nothing for them to say, those who wallow in evil.

God? Once and for all: for carnal love God doesn't care at all. His name joined with or set against the beloved — it doesn't matter which, male or female — sounds sacrilegious. They are incommensurable things, Christ and carnal love. God has nothing to do with all these afflictions; at best he can cure us of them. For He said, once and for all time: "Love me, the eternal one. Apart from that, all is vanity." Complete and utter vanity. By the very fact alone that I love a human being with this love, I betray Him, who died for me and for others on the cross of that other love.

Church and State? They can't dare say a word, until they stop prodding and blessing thousands of young men into killing each other off.

And what could be said, is being said by nature, the only avenger and defender of our physical deviations. Nature says: No. In forbidding us this, it defends itself. God, forbidding us something, does it out of love for us; nature, forbidding it, does it for love of itself, for hatred of everything which is not itself. Nature hates a monastery as much as the island upon which washed the head of Orpheus. In its vengeance we perish. True, in a monastery we have God to help us; there, on the island, is only the sea to drown in.

Island: a part of land that is yet not land, a land that it's not given one to abandon, a land that you must love once you're condemned to it. A place whence all can be seen, whence nothing can be done.

A land that can be reckoned by paces. Cul-de-sac.

The great sufferer, who was a great poetess, chose her birthplace well.

The lepers' brotherhood.

Beyond nature. Yet, how does it happen, then, that a young girl, this natural creature, so intently, so trustingly, gets off the track?

The soul's trap. Falling into the arms of the older one, she falls not into a trap of nature, nor that of the beloved, who all too often is considered a temptress, a huntress, a bird of prey — and even a vampire, whereas almost invariably she is but a grieving and noble creature, whose only crime is that she foresees too much, and (truth be told) foresees separation. The young girl falls into the soul's trap.

She wants to love — but... she would love passionately — were it not... and now in the arms of the other, head on breast, where dwells the *soul.*

Push her off? Let's ask men, young and old.

And then — the meeting. Unexpected and inevitable for — even if they live from now on in different worlds — the earth upon which they tread is anyhow the same.

Jolt of heart, surge and ebb of blood. And a woman's first and last weapon — the one with which she disarms, with which she hopes to disarm even death — the pitiful, ultimate bravery — quivering and already scarlet blade — the smile. Then a meek and disconnected torrent of syllables, lapping over each other like tiny ripples of water over stones. What did she say? Nothing, for the other one heard nothing, since usually we hear nothing of first words. But now see how the other, tearing her eyes off the moving lips, realizes that there is meaning in their movement: "... ten months ... love ... he prefers me to all the rest ... he is a man of substance ... (Take that and that and once again that, take it all — for all you've done to me!) ... So, I was saying — of substance ... (And its weight is greater than the entire earth, greater than all the seas on the heart of the older woman.)

What a pleasure her revenge! And in her eyes what hatred! Hatred of a slave at long last released. The pleasure of stomping on a heart.

And now, the meek torrent is ultimately barred — languid, melodious, lapping, crystal waves: 'Perhaps you'll pay us a visit someday, me, us, my husband and me ...' "

She's forgotten nothing. On the contrary, she remembers too much.

And then the bath, daily, sacred rite. The evident — and almost indecent — triumph of virility. Because it is — a son, right away a son, always a son, as though nature, hurrying to reclaim its rights, doesn't waste time with the roundabout route of a girl. Not the little *she*, prayed for and unattainable: a tiny he, coming on his own, unbidden, according to plan, simple consequence (of an immense design).

The other woman, clinging to the last hope, or simply not knowing what to say: "He looks like you." "No" (curtly and clearly). A *name*, curtly and clearly. And the last stab — and with it perhaps the last trace of that great venom that is love:

"He looks like his father. The absolute copy of my husband." There is deliberate crudeness in this revenge. She picks the words that — she knows this — will be most offensive, most banal, most crass (see what a mediocrity you loved!). Intent or instinct? It all rolls out of her as if by itself, she hears herself speaking (as one day long ago she heard herself laughing ...). Then, the ritual concluded, Moses saved and swaddled, she gives him her breast and — oh, highest revenge — she lurks in wait behind lowered lashes for the glittering envy in the eyes of the older woman, drowning in a sea of affection. For there is in the heart of every woman, unless she is not a monster, for there is in the heart of every monster ..., for there are no monsters among women.

This glitter, this smile — she *knows* them, but — for this or another reason — she will not raise her eyes.

A man, if he is intelligent, never will ask: "What are you thinking?"

Perhaps, the other departed, she will want to smash her own head.

Perhaps, the other departed, she will spurn his kisses.

A man, if he is intelligent, won't embrace her immediately: he'll wait — to embrace her — until the other leaves — for good.

(Why had she come? To cause herself pain? Sometimes the single thing we have left.) And then — another encounter, reencounter, reprisal, and then — *reckoning*.

The same place (nothing else is worth mentioning, since everything that happens happens within).

The same audience. (Nature's last revenge: for having been too alone, too autonomous, too everything for each other, from now on they will see each other only with everybody and everything between them.)

The same time: eternity of youth, while it *lasts*.

"Look, isn't that your friend?" "Where?" "There, with the brunette in the blue dress."

She knows without looking.

And now the human wave, more inhuman and ineluctable than those of the sea, carries her, draws her to her . . .

This time the older one starts: "How are You doing?" (and, without waiting, without listening) "May I introduce You to my friend, Mademoiselle So-and-so. . . (a name).

If the former, all of whose blood at once ebbs from her rouged cheeks "was" a blonde, the new one, the replacement, invariably will be a brunette. Essence of grace. Essence of might. Posthumous fidelity? Craving a final death? Memory's last *coup de grâce*? Resentment for all blondes? Killing the blonde with the brunette? It's the law. Ask men why.

There are stares that kill. But not this time, since the brunette is already drifting away, vivacious on the arm of the older one, the beloved one. Wrapped in the blue waves of her long dress that physically puts between she who stays and she who goes the irreversibility of the ocean.

At night, leaning over the sleeping, the adorable: "Ah, Jean, if you only knew, if you only knew, if you only knew . . ."

Not, then, on the day he was born, but today, three years later, she understands what he has cost her.

Till the other one grows old, she will always be accompanied by a living shadow.

The brunette will change, becoming again a blonde or maybe a redhead. The brunette will go away, the way the blonde went, the way all women go, toward their unknown destination — always the same — lingering for a moment to rest under the tree that never goes.

They all will pass this way. They all *would have passed this way* were it not... were it not... were it not... But eternal youth is given to nobody.

The other! Let's think about her. The island. The eternally isolated. A mother losing one by one all her daughters forever, for they not only won't come to her with their children, to put them in her arms, but if they notice her at an intersection they will stealthily put the sign of the cross upon the little blonde heads. Niobe with her feminine brood, devastated by this other hunter, fierce in a different way. Always losing in the only worthwhile (the only) game. Disgraced, exiled, and cursed. White, incorporeal specter, whose kind is known only by her gaze: recognizing, comprehending, appraising — auctioneer merges with idol worshipper, chess player with one who's sampled ecstasy; it's a gaze of layered depth, the last one always turning into the last but one: without end, without limit. Here all definitions fail, for this is an abyss. Ineffable gaze, effaced by the winter smile of rejection.

When they are young, they are known by their smile; when they age, though they smile, no one wants to know them.

Whether old or young, the visage of these women, more than to anything else, is akin to the soul. All the others, whose appearance is body, *are not this*, are not of this, or are but in passing.

She lives on an island. She creates an island. She is an island. Island with an infinite colony of souls. Who knows, maybe at this very moment, somewhere out there in India, at the earth's edge... a young girl plaiting her dark hair...

The "who knows" instills hope.

And this breeds certitude.

She'll die alone for she is too proud to love a dog and remembers too much to adopt someone's child. She wants no animals, no orphans, no lady companions around her. She doesn't want even a girl companion. King David, who warmed himself in the soulless warmth of Abishag, was coarse and crass. She doesn't want warmth for hire or a borrowed smile. She wants to be neither a vampire nor a grandmother. Lucky for the man whose old age is satisfied with leftovers, with shouldering up to any shoulders, backing against any backs, smiles flying to other lips — arrested, stolen at random. "Pass by, girls, pass by ..." She will never be a poor relative at the feast of others' youth. Neither friendship, nor esteem, nor that other abyss, our own kindness — she will put nothing in the place of love. She won't renounce the splendid blackness, the black charred hole — circle — magical one, but different from your circle, Faust! — of the fires of past joy. Against every springtime she will stand firm.

Even if some young girl flings herself at her, the way a child flings itself at a passerby or a wall: a passerby, she'll back away; a wall, she won't stir. That once ferocious lover, in old age will remain pure — out of pride. Able all her life to frighten, she wouldn't like to frighten in this manner. The young demoness will never become an old lamia.

Kindness — condescension — detachment.

"Pass by, ye raving and beautiful ..."

Under crumbling, under sullied,
Under ravaged fortress walls,
Raising hands against the sunlight,
Pass by, maidens, pass by, gals.

And yet, all the same, he — in the sanctioned halo of all their past blondeness, passes he. She — in a haze of horror.

What neither God, nor man, nor even her own compassion could do to her, to her fatal and natural proclivity, her pride will do. And will do it alone. And will do it so well that some girl — eternal youth — all affright, will cling to her mother: "That lady makes me scared. She looks so severe. What have I done to offend her? ..."

And another, when her mother will lead her to "the lady" (who knows why?), will hear her voice crack with controlled agitation: "Your mother tells me you have a talent for painting. One should certainly cultivate one's talents, Mademoiselle ..."

Never powdered, never painted, never made-up to look young, to look false, she will leave that to "normal" old hags, who, in their sixties, in broad daylight, blessed by a priest, get married to twenty-year-olds. She will leave all that to Caesar's sisters.

Fatal, natural pull of the mountain to the valley and the stream to the lake ...

When evening approaches, the mountain starts to flow back to the summit.

When evening falls, it merges with the summit. As though its streams carry it upward. And when evening descends, the mountain absorbs itself.

And one day the one who once upon a time was junior learns that somewhere, at the opposite end of the very same earth, the other woman has died. First she'll want to write to confirm it. But time will rush on, the letter won't advance. The desire will remain a desire. The "I want to know" will become "I would like to"; later "I would like not to." What for, since she is dead? Since I too will die someday . . . And resolutely, with all the great honesty of indifference: "After all, didn't she die in me — for me — twenty years ago?"

In order to be dead, it's not imperative to die.

Island. Summit. Aloneness.

Weeping willow! Sobbing willow! Willow: women's body and soul. Sobbing neck of willow. Gray hair tousled across the face, in order to see nothing more. Gray hair sweeping the earth's face.

Water, air, mountains, trees are given to us to comprehend the human soul, hidden so deeply. When I see the way a willow weeps, I understand Sappho.

Clamart, Nov. –Dec. 1932
(Recopied and revised November 1934,
with a few more gray hairs. MT)

Translated by Edwina J. Cruise

EDWINA J. CRUISE is a professor of Russian at Mount Holyoke College, Massachusetts.

The Unmeeting

"J'ai lu Votre livre," the Russian poet Marina Tsvetaeva (1892–1941) wrote, in French, in October 1932. She is addressing Natalie Clifford Barney (1877–1971), a French writer, American by birth, and one of the most extraordinary and famous women of her time. Natalie Barney was not simply a feminist, agitating for women to be granted the same rights as men to build their own destiny. She was also one of the very few women of that era to realize the aims of women's liberation and to live her own life in accord with those convictions. Barney was doubtless assisted by her father's generous inheritance, which made possible her financial independence, but even before his death she had taken up residence in Europe and set out on her own.

Her first book, *Quelques Portrait-Sonnets de Femmes,* appeared in 1900. In verses explicitly extolling lesbian love, she made public her own sexual preferences. In both her life and her art Barney was a celebrant of Sapphic love; she was often described as "the queen of lesbians." She composed her own epitaph, in which she called herself "the friend of men and the lover of women."

Miss Barney owes her current reputation to her close friend, the famous poet, novelist, and essayist Rémy de Gourmont, founder of the journal Mercure de France and one of France's first modern literary critics. In 1912–13 Gourmont's journal published his "Lettres à l'Amazone,", which had been inspired by Barney and was dedicated to her. These letters gave Barney the name she was to use henceforth among her friends, as well as in her writing; two of her books are called *Pensées d'une Amazone* (1918, 1920) and *Nouvelles Pensées de l'Amazone* (1939). A second volume of Gourmont's diaries, *Lettres intimes à l'Amazone,* appeared in 1926, ten years after his death.

It was Gourmont who helped Barney launch at her home on rue Jacob the literary salon that met regularly from 1909 to 1968. Every week on Fridays writers, poets, artists (and occasionally musicians) gathered there from every corner of the globe. Among her guests were women writers and artists, feminists like their hostess; with a number of them she shared an intimate relationship. Her male guests included several leading intellectuals. At various times her salon was frequented by Anatole France, Marcel Proust, Rainer Maria Rilke, T.S. Eliot, Ezra Pound, Paul Valéry, Romaine Brooks, Gertrude Stein, Djuna Barnes, and many others. Miss Barney became a living legend; she, her circle of friends, and her sexual life were the basis for Radcliffe Hall's *The Well of Loneliness* and Djuna Barnes's *Ladies Almanack,* both published in 1928.

But who was Marina Tsvetaeva? In the West she is now remembered, if only by hearsay, as one of the century's great poets. But at the time, in the early thirties, her name was familiar only to Russians and then only in the small circle of literary figures and lovers of poetry.

Tsvetaeva was among the poorest of Russian émigré intellectuals living in Paris. Wife of a former White army officer and mother of two children, she was the main breadwinner of her family. She struggled mightily to feed and educate her children, but that might was not enough. In her own world, the world of the Spirit, she, the Poet, could do all things. But here on earth, in the everyday world, there was nothing she could accomplish, even though she did everything that was required. She went to market (at the end of the day when shopkeepers reduced their prices), cooked, cleaned, washed the floors, and stoked the stove. Only after she had met all her family responsibilities would Tsvetaeva allow herself to write.

She worked a great deal and produced a rich yield, in a variety of genres: lyric verse and poems, tragedies based on classical themes, literary-philosophical essays and memoirs. There were, however, few opportunities to be printed in Russian émigré publications; the reading public barely exceeded the number of contributing writers. Furthermore, Tsvetaeva never wrote on commission, but only on orders from within herself. She staunchly asserted her creative independence and would not tolerate compromise; her straightforward and candid manner often alienated her from the very persons on whom she depended for earnings. She was not helped in this regard by the actively pro-Soviet positions of her husband, Sergey Efron, a member of the "Union for Return to the Motherland" later exposed as an agent of the KGB and an accessory to several political assassinations.

Over time Tsvetaeva felt increasingly alone. In 1925 Tsvetaeva wrote to her dear friend and brother-in-verse Boris Pasternak: "... they don't like poetry here, but without that — not so much the poetry, but whence it comes — who am I? An ungracious hostess, a young woman in worn clothes." Six or seven years later, when

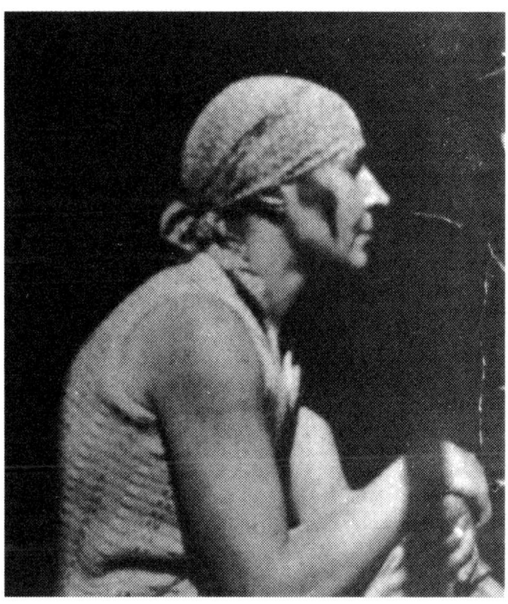

Marina Tsvetaeva, 1932.

Tsvetaeva met Natalie Clifford Barney, she was no longer so young and her clothes were even more worn.

Tsvetaeva was brought to Barney's salon by Hélène Iswolsky, the first translator of Pasternak's poetry into French. When Tsvetaeva's fortunes were at their lowest, Iswolsky attempted to organize support for her, and solicited funds from émigré Russians of means. Tsvetaeva was indeed in need of assistance. Her French had always been as good as her Russian, and she had been hoping to break into print in that language. This would expand her readership and provide her with much-needed income. In the fall of 1930 Tsvetaeva had completed a translation into French of her fairy tale in verse "Molodets" ("Le Gars") and was seeking a publisher. Miss Barney was known as a patron of the arts and, as Iswolsky recalls, she was "very influential in the Paris literary world. A word of recommendation from

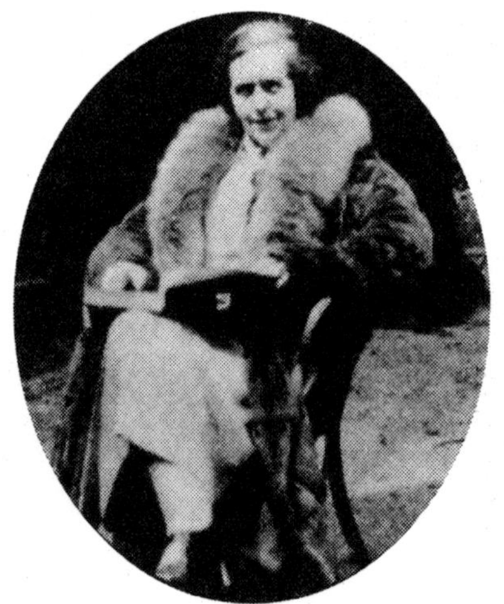

Natalie Clifford Barney, circa 1930.

her ... was an 'open Sesame' to the door of every important literary periodical."

On the day Tsvetaeva was to read in Barney's salon, there were no celebrities present. "Marina read her poems in her brilliant, precise French translation, and with perfect diction, but the audience gave her no more than a cool reception."[1] Neither "the woman in the worn dress" nor her poetry aroused the interest of the salon's hostess. Publication in French of Tsvetaeva's poetry never materialized. She did not visit Miss Barney again, but it was most likely this encounter that prompted Tsvetaeva to read *Pensées d'une Amazone* and to write her own "Lettre à l'Amazone" to its author.

Barney's book, which Ezra Pound called "interesting as documentary evidence of a specimen liberation,"[2] incited Tsvetaeva — she was scarcely indifferent to its theme. At one time in her youth, in a life now past, she had had a passionate affair with the poetess Sofiya Parnok, an affair in which she suffered terribly and which she later called her "first catastrophe." That passion found expression in a large poem cycle, "The Friend," which capped the youthful period of her artistic development and paved the way for her mature work. *Pensées d'une Amazone*'s talk of love between women awakened these memories and feelings in Tsvetaeva. It is this personal experience that makes "Lettre à l'Amazone" so intimate in its passion and, I would even say, so impassioned in its convictions. Written in the form of a letter, this lyrical-philosophical essay goes far beyond the conventions of personal correspondence. Just as Barney had, Tsvetaeva probes to the very core of love between two women, analyzes it, and comes to the conclusion that it is tragically irreconcilable with the nature of a woman.

Tsvetaeva her whole life sought "a kindred soul" and for many years regarded physical intimacy as a means to overcome the limits of "the corporeal" and to penetrate the soul of the beloved: she spoke about that often and it was present in her verse. And now, in "Lettre à l'Amazone," she subscribes to this point of view — that a "young girl falls into the soul's trap." The younger woman fears men, she has no need of "the corporeal," she seeks "a kindred soul" and finds it in an older woman. This is the "soul's trap" into which the older woman, doomed by deathful loneliness, lures the younger. Thus begins, in Tsvetaeva's thinking, their amorous bond. For a certain time their relationship creates a harmony of "the corporeal" and "the spiritual," but there soon arises an awareness of the impossibility of a Child: this leads to the tragic end of every such pairing. Tsvetaeva naïvely thought that she was dealing a blow not only personally to the author of *Pensées d'une Amazone,* but also to the convictions to which Barney devoted her life.

A few years after she wrote "Lettre à l'Amazone," Tsvetaeva returned to the theme of homoerotic love in a private letter to the Russian poet and critic Yury Ivask. Again she dwelled on the tragic character of this kind of relationship, on the "specialness of this species," on the restrictiveness of this circle and its obligatory togetherness — on "caste," what in "Lettre à l'Amazone" she called "the lepers' brotherhood" and "the horror of this curse." But now her view of the connection between the spiritual and the erotic had changed; personal experience had convinced her that, irrespective of sexual issues, any such union was virtually impossible. Specifically in the context of her letter to Ivask, himself a homosexual, she asserts that male homosexuals are not capable of friendship with each other: "*Your* [kind] are *not* capable of *male friendship*." Based on her contact with members of that "caste," she had concluded that they can only engage in friendship with women. As in "Lettre à l'Amazone," Tsvetaeva speaks with pity of the tragic illusions of even the "best" of this "caste," those for whom homosexuality is not a game but an innate proclivity. Of those for whom this is a game "I say nothing at all, and if I should speak, then only with absolute contempt; they are manipulators of *living* souls, seducers of the defenseless — regardless of the sex to which they belong."

The papers of Natalie Clifford Barney contain neither mention of Marina Tsvetaeva nor the text of her "Lettre à l'Amazone." Although there is no evidence to confirm that Miss Barney read the essay or even that Tsvetaeva sent it to her, scholars have found its echoes in Barney's later works, *Nouvelles Pensées d'une Amazone* (1939) and *Traits et portraits* (1963).

Natalie Clifford Barney lived a long, comfortable, and quiet life, replete with romantic affairs with women and interesting meetings with men. During World War II, when she was living in Italy, she became an anti-Semite and openly supported Italian fascism. Marina Tsvetaeva, a dutiful wife and mother, followed her husband and daughter back to Russia in 1939. Two months after her return, her daughter was arrested, and a month later so was her husband. At the beginning of the war, Tsvetaeva was evacuated to the small town of Elabug, where she hanged herself. Her son perished at the front at age nineteen.

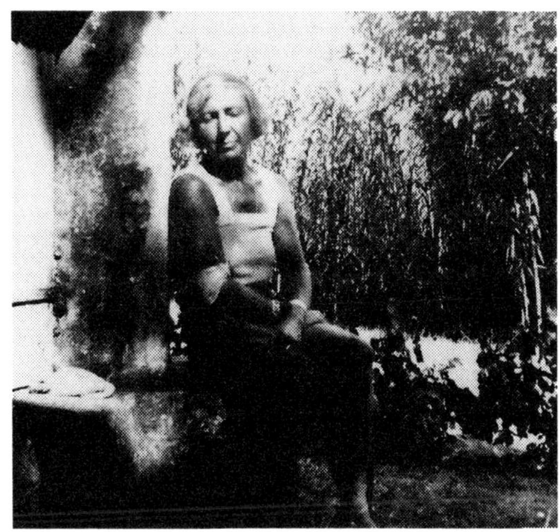

Marina Tsvetaeva, 1932.

"Lettre à l'Amazone" was first published in Mercure de France in 1979, under the title "Mon frère féminin: Lettre à l'Amazone."

Viktoria Schweitzer

[1] Iswolsky, Hélène, *No Time to Grieve: An Autobiographical Journey* (Philadelphia: Winchell, 1985), pp. 199–200.

[2] Quoted in George Wicks, *The Amazon of Letters* (New York: G.P. Putnam's Sons, 1976), p. 160.

VIKTORIA SCHWEITZER is a lecturer at Mount Holyoke College and Amherst College. She is the author of *Tsvetaeva. A Biography*.

EIGHT POEMS

LARS GUSTAFSSON

Early memories, fume from childhood,
green bits of bottleglass
dug from earth.

*

In School
The letters
and the dreadful pain they cost fingers
and the hand having to write them
with a nib of steel.

*

The soft steps of the horses
in the dark of night.

One single apple falls.
Hoofs on mud.

And the person who took a pee
comes back to the warmth of the house.

*

How does the water know the boat is coming?
In certain positions
especially with a wind astern
it dips visibly
before the bow

☆

When the jet
tows its invisible stone crate

across the limpid autumn sky

for a moment in their creek the minnows
shiver with fear.

Clocks tick tentatively in tropical rooms.

Time takes the children with it, makes them grow.

Where the children stood, suddenly silence.

☆

Dry flies
almost weightless on the smooth
black surface:

and the ability to say just this

☆

Elegy on Objects Mislaid and Forgotten

The gloves that ended undermost in a drawer.
The old brass lure beneath a sea of screws.

And a hammer, flakes of mortar on its handle,
surely part of the family since 1939,

but now the earth has swallowed it up, like that.
All these things that were close to us once

now must recall unhelped their whereabouts,
mustn't depend on me but go it alone.

I still know how they looked, sense them in my hand,
even remember the hammer on a Sunday

in the distant forties, when I was too little
to lift it properly,

and with what care my father took it from me.

The world, a labyrinth of objects

mislaid and forgotten, from the ancient swords
in never opened graves of the Bronze Age

to the bifocals that vanished yesterday,
retains them. No cause for alarm.

And you, going around in search so ardently,
might you be an object someone is looking for?

And it occurs to you, one night when a thing
turns up again, scratched and rusty, but the same,

in a box awash with bolts and padlocks,
that all this looking for objects

did no more than mirror your own craving:
that someone just as ardently might look for you.

Elegy on the Density of the World

While Nicola Pisano is carving in Pisa
reliefs out of the Baptistery marble,

evidently he knows there is a problem.
Behind every image another is lurking.

Even at sea it is so.
In Nicola's images, pushing and shoving,

Apostles, Soldiers, Horses, Wise Men,
one horse peering across another's withers.

Just so this image fills to the brim.
No help: there's always more to follow,

Apostles, Soldiers, Horses, Wise Men, more soon
surge forward, jostling one another,

there isn't marble enough in Carrara for all of it!
Children are spellbound by sieves and colanders,

drag them out of the kitchen closet, hold them up,
reverently, to the world. And see, as they do so,

Sieve and Behind-Sieve at the same time.
How dense it is, the world they drifted into!

The depth of this density horrifies us,
and isn't it strictly prohibited to dream

of standing face to face with a final image?

Or perhaps we dream of a breathing space:
being enfolded a moment in a single image,

exhaling in it. And being one with it:
image in image, briefly, still in stillness.

Till the storm breaks loose again with full force.

Translated from the Swedish by the author and Christopher Middleton

LARS GUSTAFSSON, born in 1936, is a Swedish poet, novelist and philosopher, who since 1980 has resided in Austin, Texas, where he teaches every spring semester as an adjunct professor of Germanic Studies and Philosophy at the University of Texas. Gustafsson has published numerous collections of poetry. His most recent book in English is *The Stillness of the World before Bach* (New Directions, 1988). CHRISTOPHER MIDDLETON, born in 1926, is a British poet and a Germanist, residing at the University of Texas at Austin, where he has been a professor of Germanic Studies since 1966. His latest collection of poetry is *Floating Miniatures* (Sal Press, 1995). He is also a translator of poetry.

LÜTFI ÖZKÖK

Lütfi Özkök has by now lived half his life in Sweden. He came here in 1951 without much more than his unfinished studies in urban planning and his, for the most part, unfinished poems. He incessantly worked on his poems and wrote "with an uncertain pen," always unsatisfied with results, always torn among different languages: Turkish, French, and, later, Swedish. He gained employment, made friends, and established a family life in Sweden, but never felt, or feels, at home here.

It is as a portrait photographer that Lütfi Özkök has become well known. Over the past decades, he has photographed several of the world's most prominent writers. Özkök's career as a portrait photographer began when he needed photos of authors to accompany the articles on and translations of Swedish and French poetry that he wrote for a Turkish magazine. Now you will find photos by Özkök in literary magazines and daily newspapers all over the world.

Ivar Ivask, Özkök's good friend, who faithfully gave him photo assignments, pointed out that Özkök's portraits are born out of an inner excitement, and adds that photography became Özkök's deliverance from a predicament in the suburbs that might otherwise have shattered him. Photography allowed him to travel and meet the writers he especially wanted to meet. Özkök made a film about one of the writers he most admired, René Char. There is an interesting paradox here in that the deeply rooted René Char is thoughtfully and energetically depicted by the rootless Özkök.

When Özkök approaches a writer he wants to photograph, his perspective is that of a poet and a photographer. From the start, he unarms his subjects with his exotic naïveté — exotic even for those from Turkey, his country of origin. I am uncertain whether to claim that Özkök's poetic work has given him a special sensitivity in his work as a photographer. But details such as the brilliance in Beckett's eyes, the black handkerchief in Jacques Prévert's coat pocket, the furrows in Auden's face, or the cigarette smoke emerging from between Vasko Popa's fingers are as subtly captured as are images from his poems that speak of, for instance, "rain with the pane's shattered color."

In an article about Özkök, Ivar Ivask says: "Pictures are universal. As soon as they are truly poetic they touch our most inner regions: wake a flash of recognition."

Lasse Söderberg

Translated from the Swedish by Alan Shima

LASSE SÖDERBERG is a Swedish poet and translator, and organizer of the yearly Malmö Poetry Festival. ALAN SHIMA is a lecturer in the English department at the University of Uppsala.

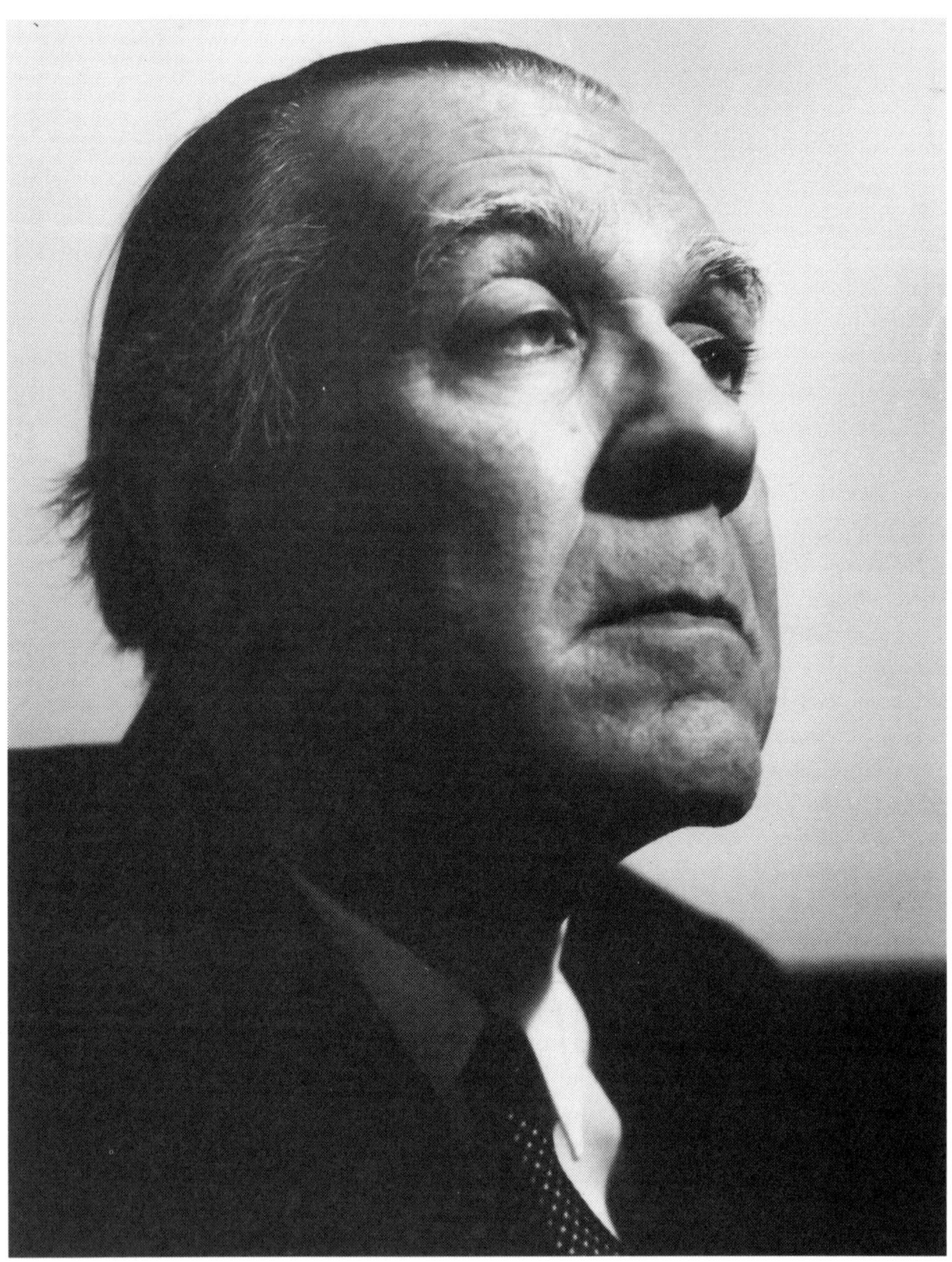

Jorge Luis Borges, 1964. © Lütfi Özkök.

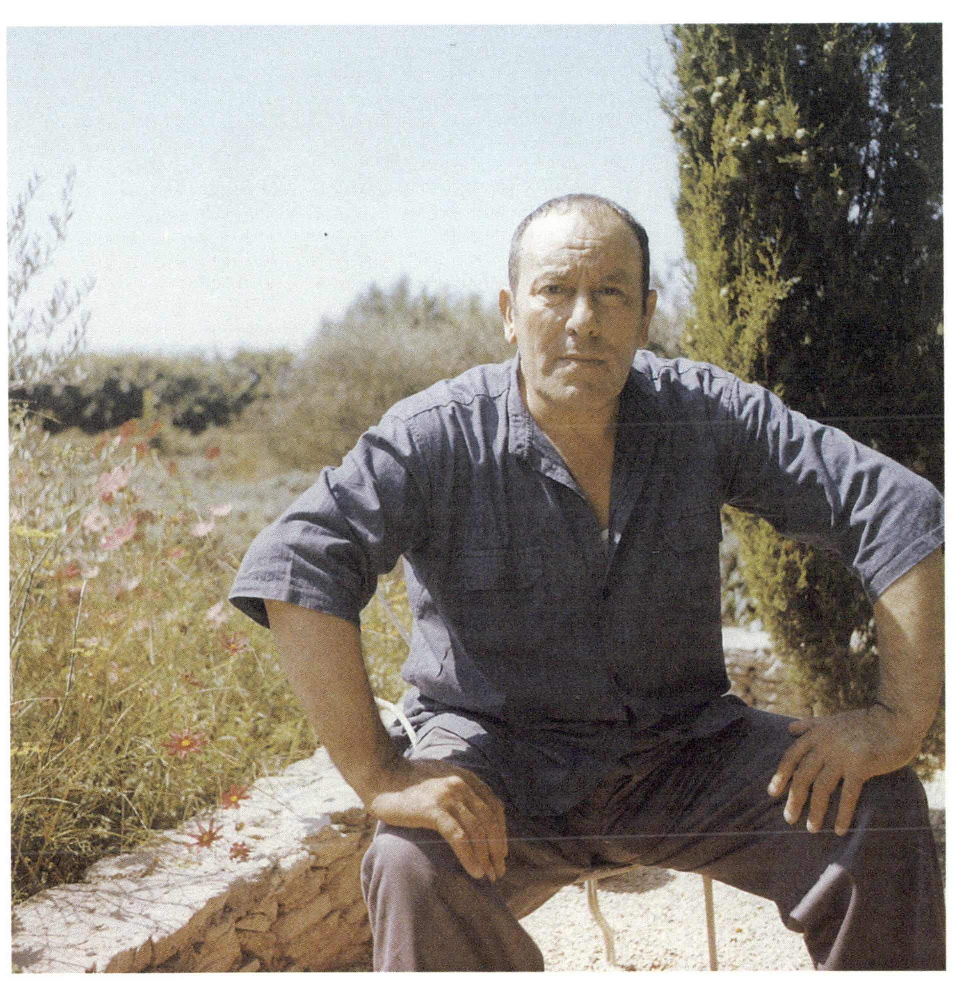

René Char, 1967. © Lütfi Özkök.

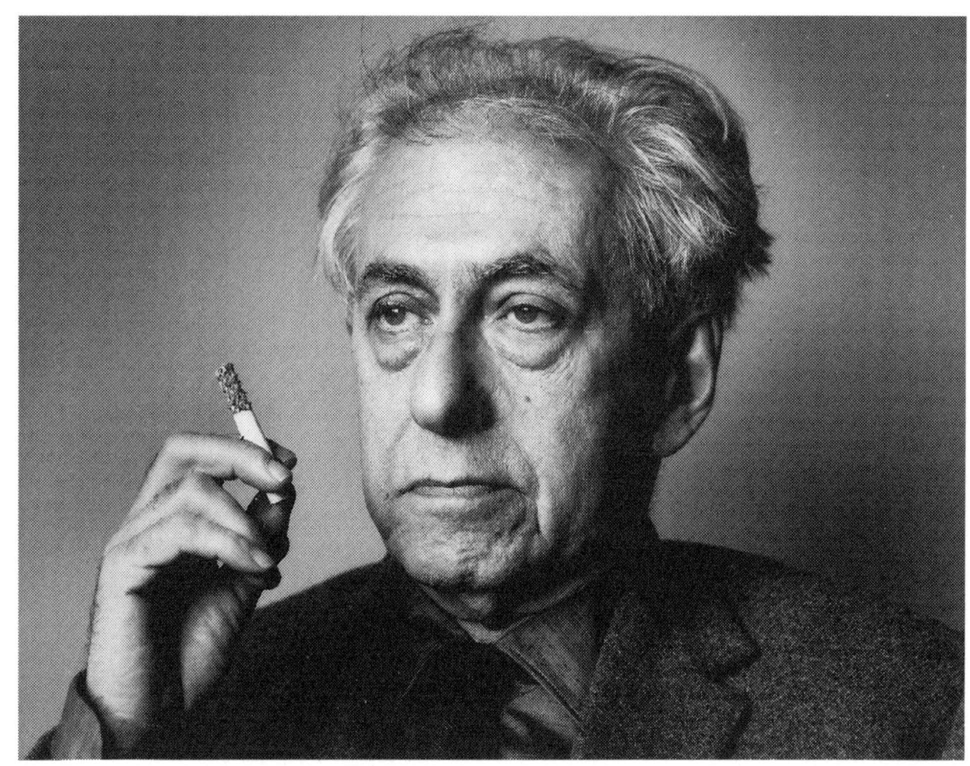

Ilya Ehrenburg, 1961. © Lütfi Özkök.

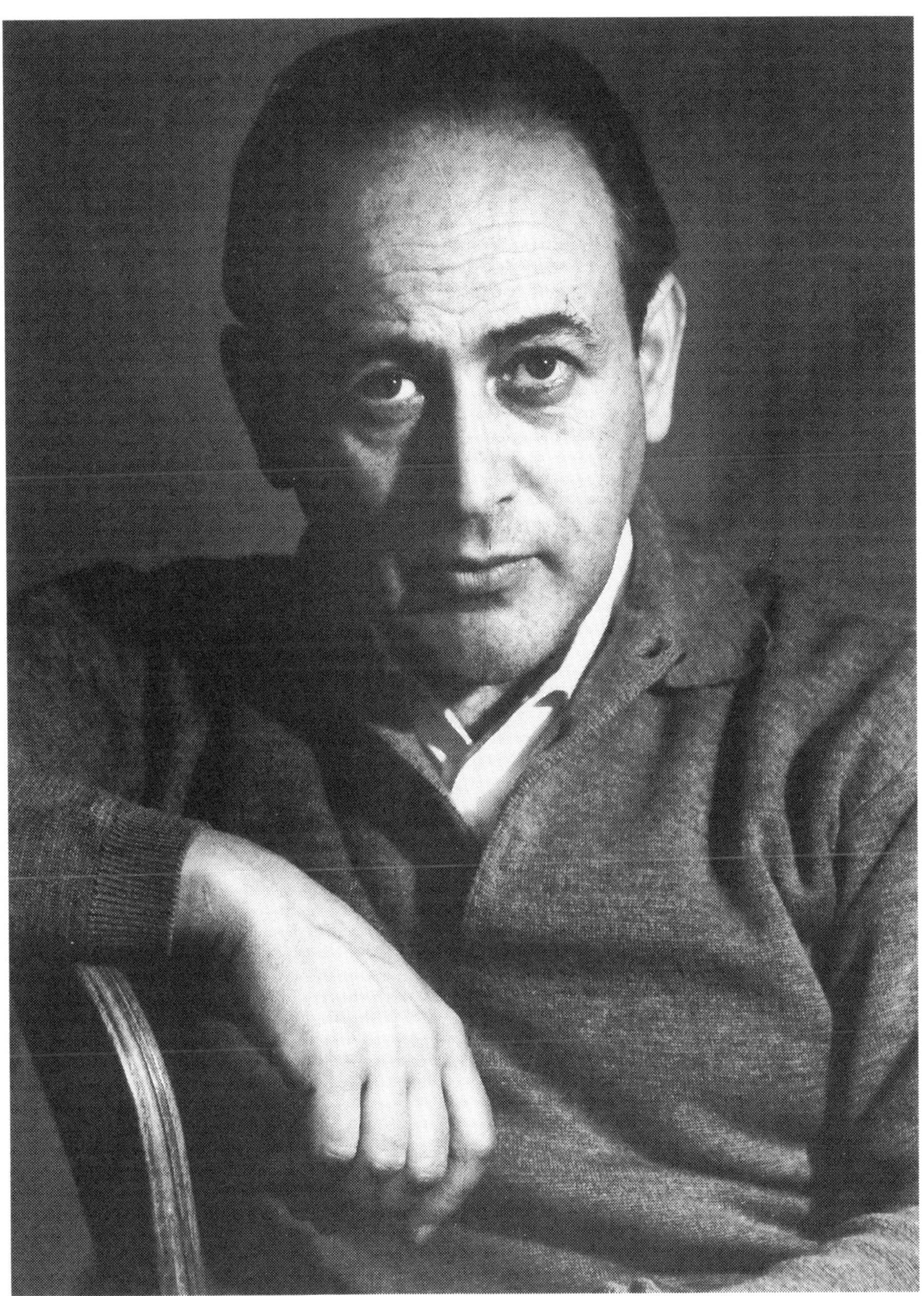

Paul Celan, 1963. © Lütfi Özkök.

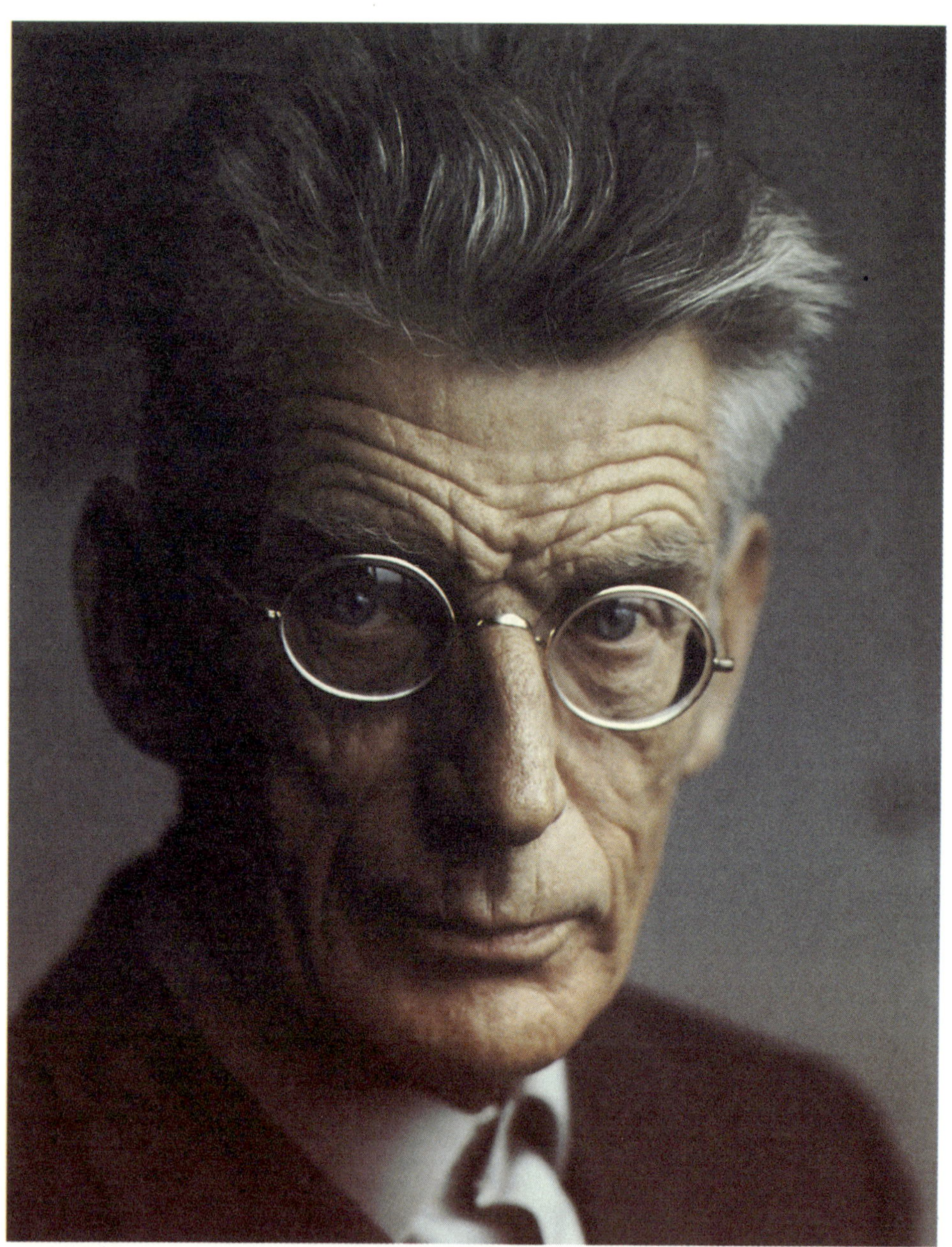

Samuel Beckett, 1966. © Lütfi Özkök.

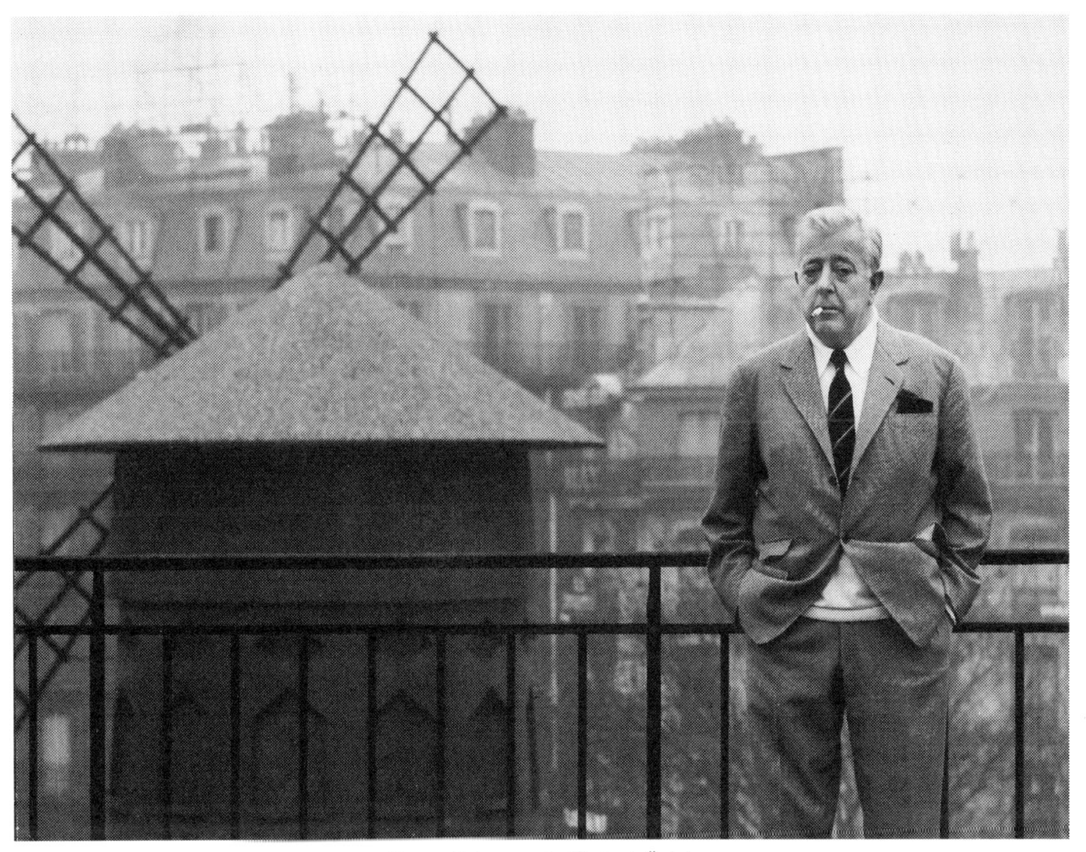

Jacques Prévert, 1961. © Lütfi Özkök.

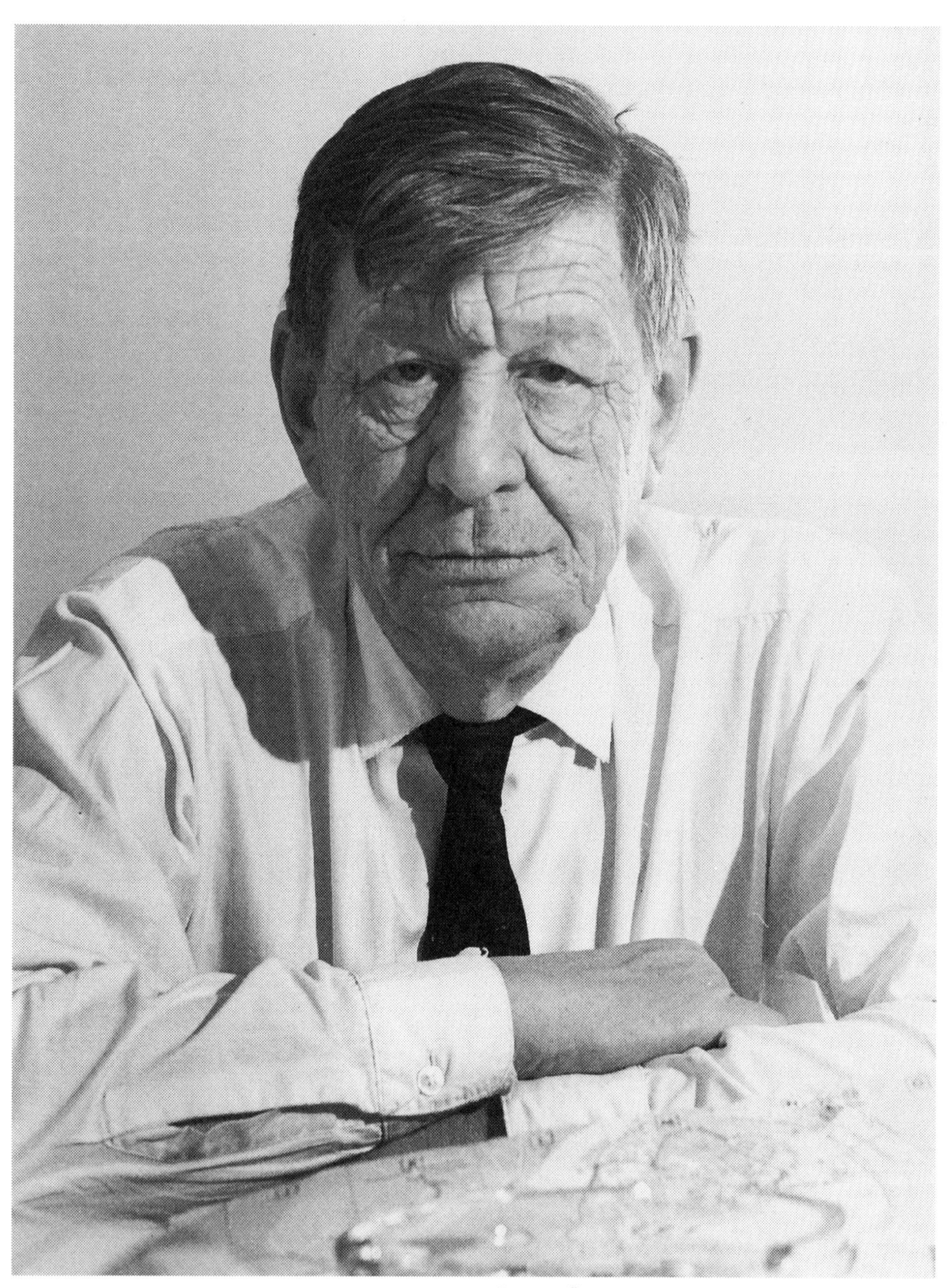

W.H. Auden, 1964. © *Lütfi Özkök.*

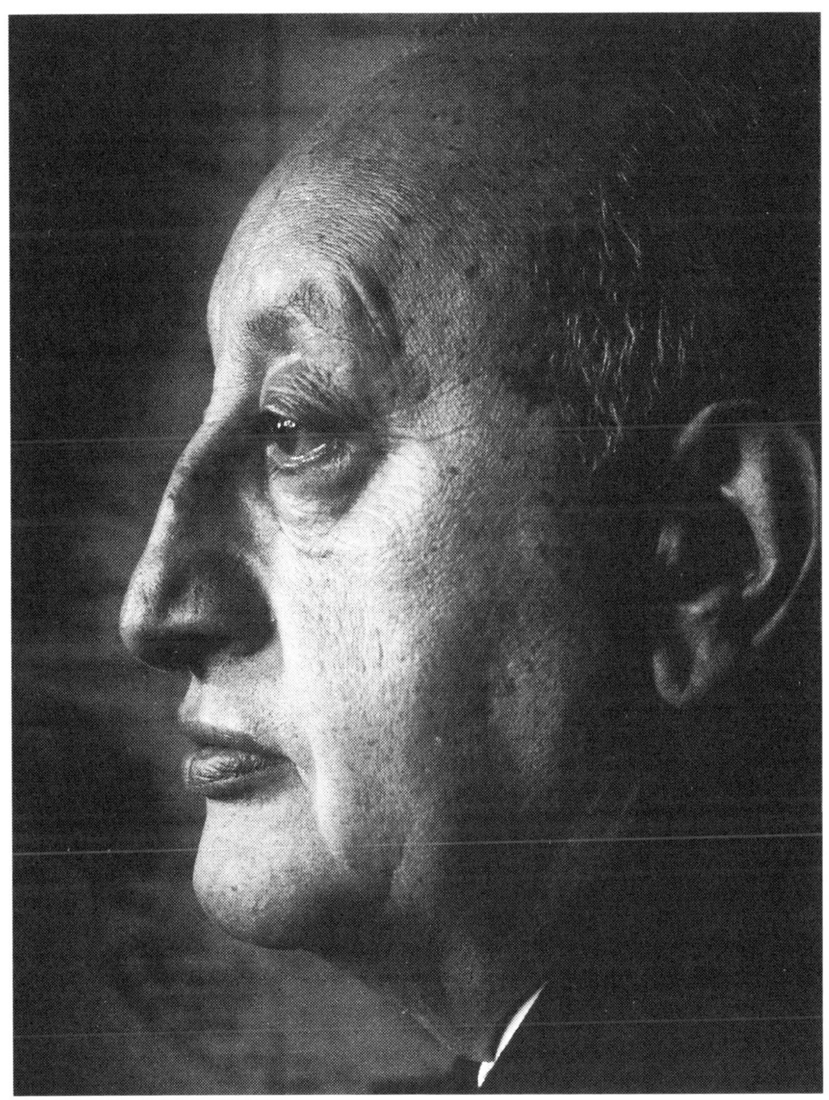

Miguel A. Asturias, 1967. © Lütfi Özkök.

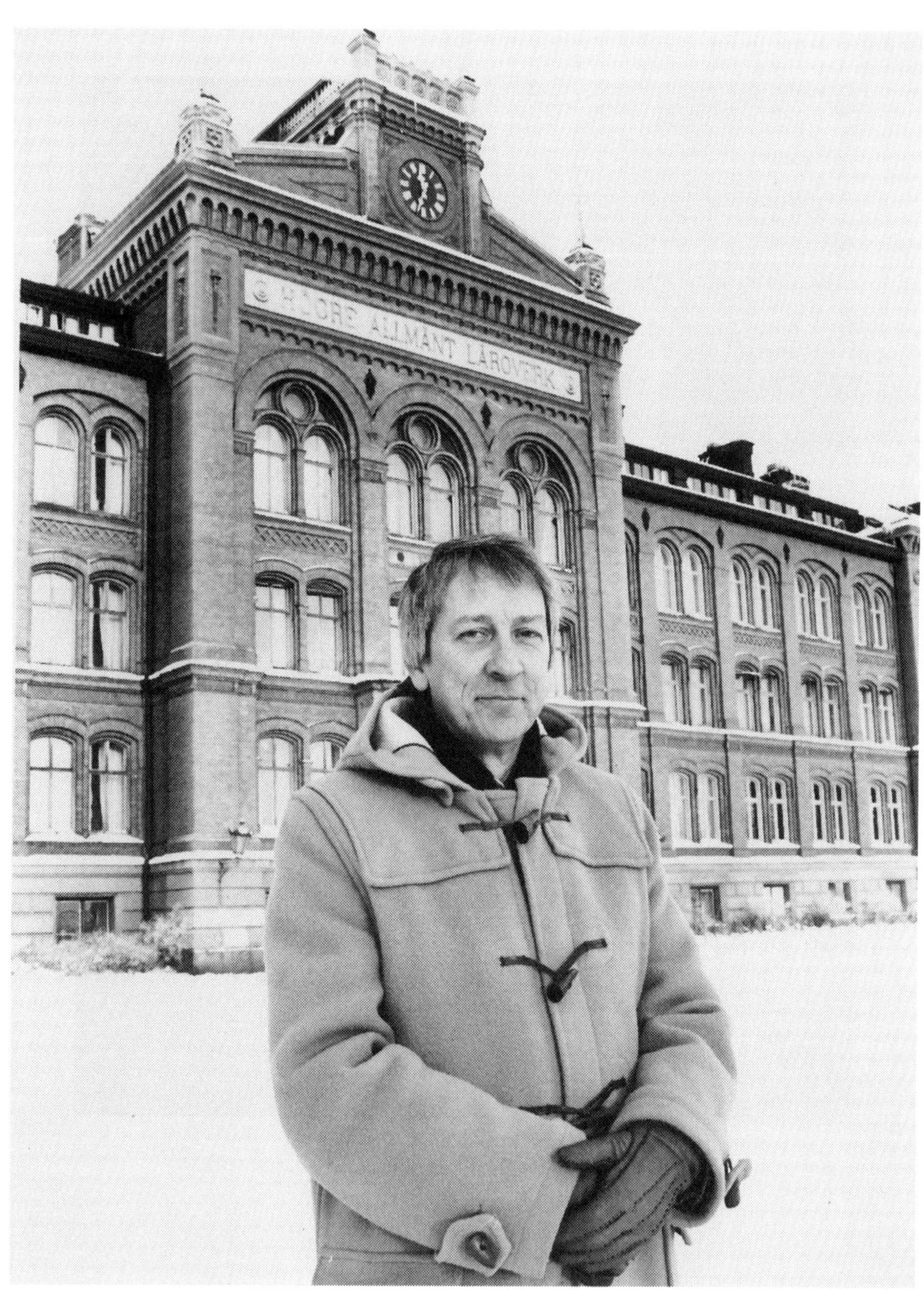

Tomas Tranströmer, 1981. © Lütfi Özkök.

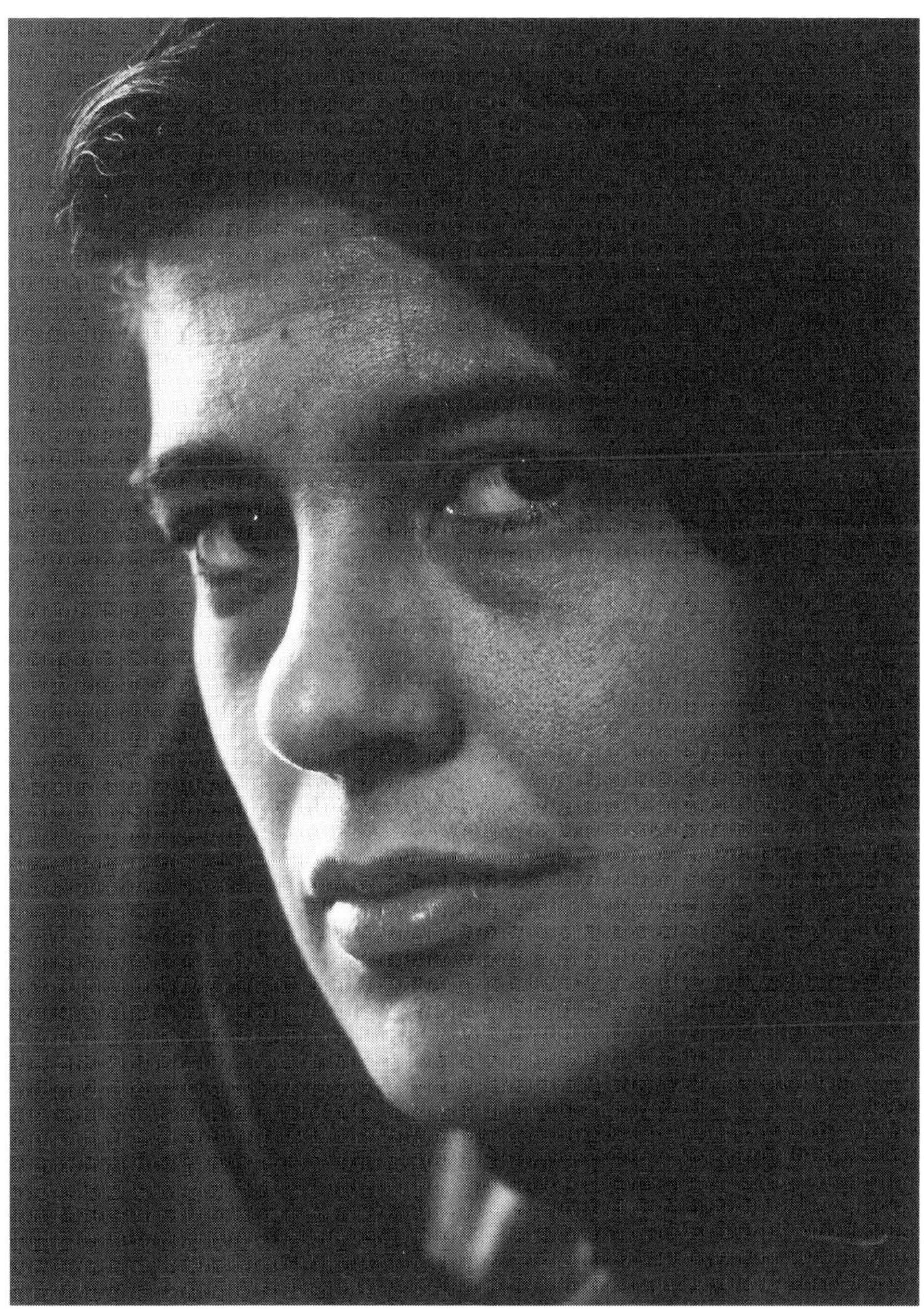

Susan Sontag, 1968. © Lütfi Özkök.

Working with Warhol

GERARD MALANGA

I worked with Andy during inarguably his most important period. The very first painting I screened was a 40" x 40" silver Elizabeth Taylor portrait at a shut-down firehouse on East 87th Street that Andy rented from the city of New York for one hundred dollars a year. In making the Elizabeth Taylor painting, masking tape was shaped to the contours of the face directly on the canvas to create a stencil that followed the lines originating from the acetate-positive. Then we filled in the flesh tones, eyebrows, and lips by hand with Liquitex. When the paint dried, the masking tape was peeled off, resulting in shaped colors. Andy remarked to me once that his paintings looked more like Alex Katz paintings before the silk-screen was applied. The last step in the process was to screen in the black paint. The paintings were a step-by-step transformation of photography into painting.

Andy loved all sorts of machines and gadgets, embracing new techniques and technologies, working with tape recorders, cassettes, and Polaroid Thermofax. But the heart of all this experimentation had as its central focus photography and the silk-screen for making a painting; this fulfilled by extension his love for the machine, because the screen process was very machinelike. Andy's reasoning was that the silk-screen would make it as easy as possible to create a painting. Ironically, the process relied directly on manual application.

When the screens were very large, we worked together; otherwise, I was pretty much left to my own inventiveness. I had a firsthand knowledge of silk-screen technique, having worked for a summer as intern to a textile chemist in the manufacture of men's neckwear, so I knew what I was doing from the start.

Andy and I would lay the screen down on the canvas, trying to line up the registration with the marks we'd made where the screen would go. Then oil-base paint was poured into a corner of the screen's frame, and I would push the paint across the mesh surface with a squeegee. Andy would grab the squeegee still in motion and continue the process of pressuring the paint through the screen from his end. We'd lift the screen, and I would swing it away from the painting and start cleaning it with paper towels soaked in a substance called Varnolene. If this was not done immediately, the remaining paint would dry and clog the pores.

After work was completed, we would go over to Andy's house. The firehouse was three blocks from where Andy lived with Julia, his mother, a seemingly frail but hearty woman who was then in her seventies. She would make lunch for us, which usually consisted of a Czechoslovakian-

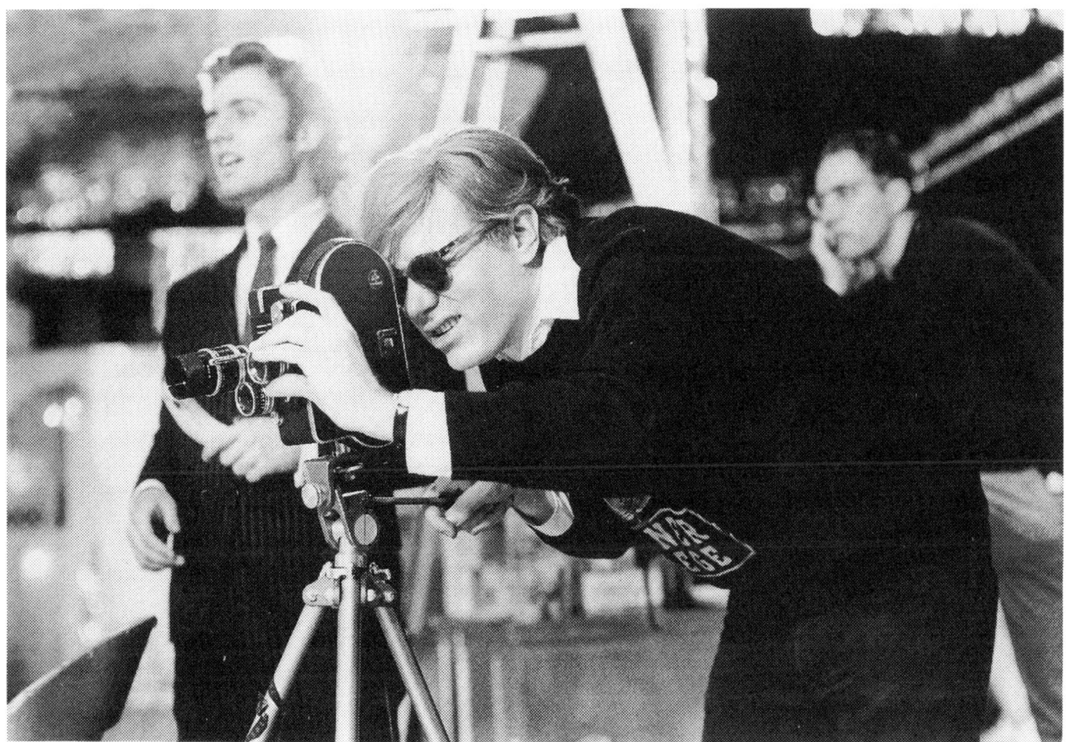

Gerard Malanga and Andy Warhol during the shooting of Couch, *1964. © Archives Malanga.*

style hamburger stuffed with diced onions, sprinkled with parsley, and always on white bread, with a 7-Up on ice.

Sometimes, he would have people over to view the work. Most of the paintings were rolled up in the corner of a very cluttered living room. He couldn't store the art at the firehouse, because there was no electricity or running water — no conveniences of any kind. The firehouse was basically a shell of a space. There was an opening in the floor where the slide-pole would have been. All this would shortly change.

In September of 1963, he was notified that the building would be put on the auction block. We went hunting for a place. We spent two months looking throughout the city. We covered Hell's Kitchen and Little Italy. The move forced Andy to get a better working space. Upon moving into the new studio, which had previously been a hat factory, all socializing at Andy's home pretty much ceased. When this happened, his work schedule changed, because once he'd leave the house for the day he was out for good. There was no returning home for lunch or anything. We were now in Midtown, on the East Side. Andy would arrive at the Factory, as it was now called, noon or thereabouts. We would work on and off until 5 or 6 p.m. and then go out to party.

The first works created at the Factory were a

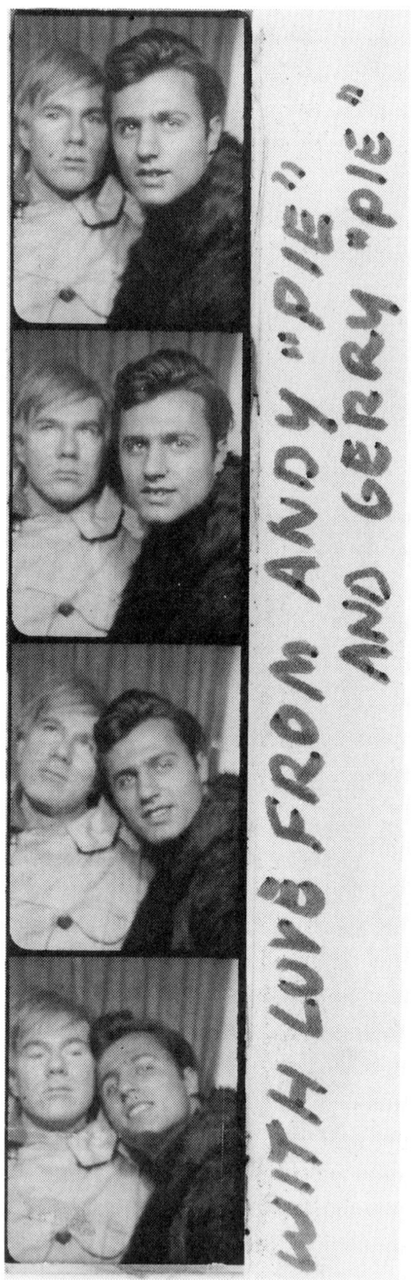

Andy Warhol and Gerard Malanga.
November 1963. © Archives Malanga.

series of food boxes. Andy was fascinated by the shelves of foodstuffs in supermarkets and the repetitive, machinelike effect they created. Andy wanted to become totally mechanical in his work, the way a packaging factory would routinely silk-screen information onto cardboard boxes. He wanted to duplicate the effect, but soon discovered that the cardboard surface was not feasible. I found a carpenter in the East Sixties, and Andy hired him to build plywood boxes that we would then paint and screen, to create the illusion of the real thing.

The brand names chosen consisted of two versions of Brillo, Heinz Tomato Ketchup, Kellogg's Corn Flakes, and Mott's Apple Sauce. We obtained cardboard-box samples of each of these products, either from a grocery store or, in the case of the Brillo box, directly from the manufacturer. I'd deliver the cardboard box, at this point flattened out, to the silk-screen manufacturer, Harry Golden, who made all of Andy's screens. Specifications were drawn up according to the size and density of the screen. In this case, we went for a total black-and-white contrast to complement the original we were working from.

We'd line up twenty or so boxes according to their size and carry the screen across their tops, one at a time. Then I'd clean the screen and turn the boxes on their sides and repeat the application until the six sides of each box were screened. We were able to get at least two sides done in a day. A hundred or more were produced in a period of a month. They were literally three-dimensional photographs of the real thing.

The ambience was workmanlike. When we were making a painting, the conversation would go something like, "Let's move it over this way." When we were working on the Elvis Presley

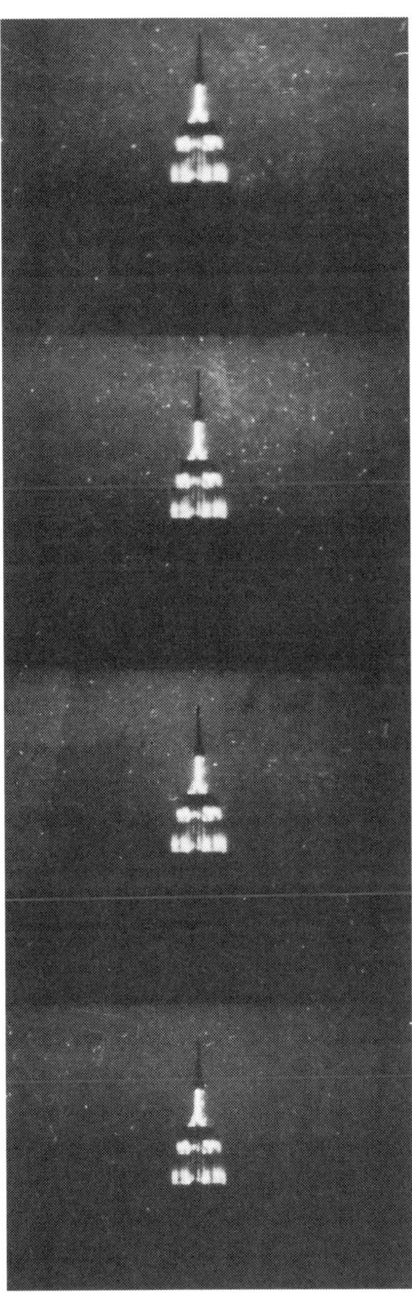

Film strip from Empire, *Summer 1964.*
© Archives Malanga.

series, I remember suggesting the superimpositions that we tried and successfully realized, which is why these paintings look the way they do. It was a creative period for both of us.

Sometimes, we'd go off-register when making a painting, and there'd be a flaw. Andy accepted these mistakes, what I would call "embracing the mistakes." We never rejected anything. If we were in the process of making a series of paintings and all of a sudden one painting went off a bit, or the image inadvertently overlapped the previous image, we kept right on moving along. We'd keep it, or, as Andy would say, "It's part of the art." He possessed an almost Zen-like sensibility.

Warhol was one of the first artists since Duchamp and the Dadaists to embrace this seemingly casual attitude. Rather than create art by hand, he made art by way of his decisions to accept or discard. Appropriative selection, as it were. He would make decisions about how certain material would go in the screen. We would discuss the possibilities. He would turn the acetate one way, then another. A decision would be reached either to go with a halftone or stick with the contrast. If we agreed, "Yeah, that's great," the screen would be ordered.

The early paintings, from 1961 to 1962, were made from screens that lacked any halftone layering. He would draw from actual photos, and the drawing would be converted into a screen that was photographic by nature to re-create the drawing as a photographic image in silk-screen application. But a year or so later, he eliminated the drawing altogether and appropriated the photo head-on, turning it into a screen. I was sometimes Andy's photo-researcher. We would discover images in newspapers and magazines, and I would search out photos in out-of-the-way, secondhand book shops, or bring something in from home.

He was still making art during the period when he started making films. In July 1963, poet-artist Charles Henri Ford and I took Andy shopping at Peerless Camera and helped him select his first movie camera — a 16 mm Bolex with through-the-lens focusing, complete with motor drive that allowed for a one-shot, three-minute take.

Sleep was Andy's first and, indisputably, his most famous film. Perhaps it was famous, too, as a film that few if any ever sat through. Andy told me, before he actually owned a movie camera, of wanting to make a film of Brigitte Bardot sleeping for eight hours. He said something to the effect that you could get to know everything there was to know about a person by watching him sleep. He wanted to know what it would be like to watch a movie star sleeping. Obviously the concept was more essential to the realization than the protagonist, and, knowing Bardot was simply out of his league, he settled for a friend, John Giorno, who was a natural for not waking up.

John gave Andy a key to his flat, and Andy would let himself in. The Bolex was already set up, with the lights in place. Andy would turn on the lights and camera, continuing to film for about two weeks.

Sleep runs approximately six and a half hours of equivalent shooting time. Andy duplicated an additional ninety minutes from an equal ninety-minute section of the film to stretch it out to eight hours, approximating the generally accepted length of time for a normal night's sleep.

The film *Empire* was also shot mostly at night in the summer of 1964. We started shooting at around 6 p.m., in the daylight, and finished at one in the morning. The first two reels are overexposed because Andy was metering for night light, but it was all guesswork. In the course of the first two reels, and partway through the third, the skyscraper slowly emerges from a twilight haze, balancing out the exposure from the darkness that slowly blankets the sky. The Empire State Building was already a star of sorts after being featured in *King Kong*, but Andy wanted to make the building an even bigger star!

Sleep and *Empire* are very similar in style. Both treat time as a one-to-one ratio. They are black and white, with no sound, shot at night, and the camera *never* moves. The only major difference between the two films is that *Sleep* was shot with the Bolex, using 100-foot/three-minute film rolls, and *Empire* was shot with a rented Auricon equipped to shoot 1,200 feet of film for thirty-five minutes, nonstop. Andy would probably have filmed *Sleep* with the Auricon had he known of the camera's existence. He was learning as he went along, mimicking the process of Hollywood without knowing it.

It was John Palmer who came up with the idea for *Empire*. Andy had the resources to get the concept realized, so he was essentially the film's producer, but he got all the credit. He barely touched the camera during the entire time the movie was being shot. John, Jonas Mekas, and I changed the reels for him. The machine would do all the work in Andy's head. So there's a direct connection between the silk-screen, which is a photographic and mechanical process, and the movie camera, which also creates a photographic-type image.

Photography has always been the underlying theme, the consistent strain in Andy's work. If you were to take a strip of 16-mm footage of *Sleep* and examine the frames horizontally, the repetitive images that occur in his head-shot paintings of Marilyn Monroe and Elvis Presley would come to mind.

I remember attending the premiere screening of *Empire* at the Bridge Cinema in Lower Manhattan. Andy and I were standing in the rear of the auditorium. He was observing the audience rather than the film, and people were walking out or booing or throwing paper cups at the screen. Andy turned to me and in his boyish voice said, "Gee, you think they hate it? You think they don't like it?" *Empire* is a seven-hour movie where nothing happens except audience reaction.

Andy was not overly conscious of how an audience might respond to one of his films. In his mind, he was realizing a concept that was perhaps less original than the decision to put that concept in motion. He extended a minimal and appropriative vocabulary to include the kind of decision-making he applied to his painting. The only way his films would be accepted or criticized was through their audiences; otherwise, they would remain concepts in a can.

Andy is often characterized as a voyeur, someone who likes to watch. Watching takes time. You don't just look and turn away; it's a matter of optic absorption. One of the ways Andy expressed obsessive looking was through the movie camera. Most of his silent films intentionally took the same amount of time to make as to watch. A voyeur needs a window frame, or a blind, if he is to inhabit a situation in a secretive way. Andy's fascination extended to watching his audience sitting in the dark. It implied power over those who are unaware of being watched, as if they were sleeping. Andy's desire for power was initially realized through the voyeuristic tendency of distancing himself from what he was watching with the use of a movie camera.

His desire to make films evolved from his love of Hollywood — the allure, magic, and mystery he responded to as an adolescent, when he wrote to film companies for photos of his favorite stars. Years later, in 1965, Andy's introduction to Edie Sedgwick was the closest he had yet come to meeting someone who possessed the aura of a Hollywood starlet.

Edie was not career-oriented at the time she met Andy. Edie was a blue blood. Her life imitated art to the extent that it was colorful and ephemeral. She had the one ingredient essential to stars — glamour. Glamour is not beauty, but it can become that. Glamour is aura. The person who already possesses an aura becomes beautiful. Andy was deeply fascinated with glamour on this level. He had an eye for it.

Edie first starred in a Warhol film with *Poor Little Rich Girl*, shot in her one-room studio. Her close friend Chuck Wein fabricated some notes and coached Edie. The concept of "embracing the mistakes" played an integral part in the film. We shot two reels. When they came back from the lab, we previewed them and, to our horror, found them to be extremely out-of-focus — not even close to salvagable. After replacing the lens, we reshot the two long takes, a week later, and got it right. We took the first reel, from the first version, and sequenced it with the second reel, from the second version, so the film opens with an out-of-focus, thirty-five minute take.

As the months progressed, Edie appeared in a number of films, some especially scripted for her, the first being *Kitchen*. The films had an instant audience; reviews ran in the press; and Edie's career was launched. She thought Andy was making money with the films, because of all the hoopla. But the sales from his paintings were supporting his highly speculative venture into

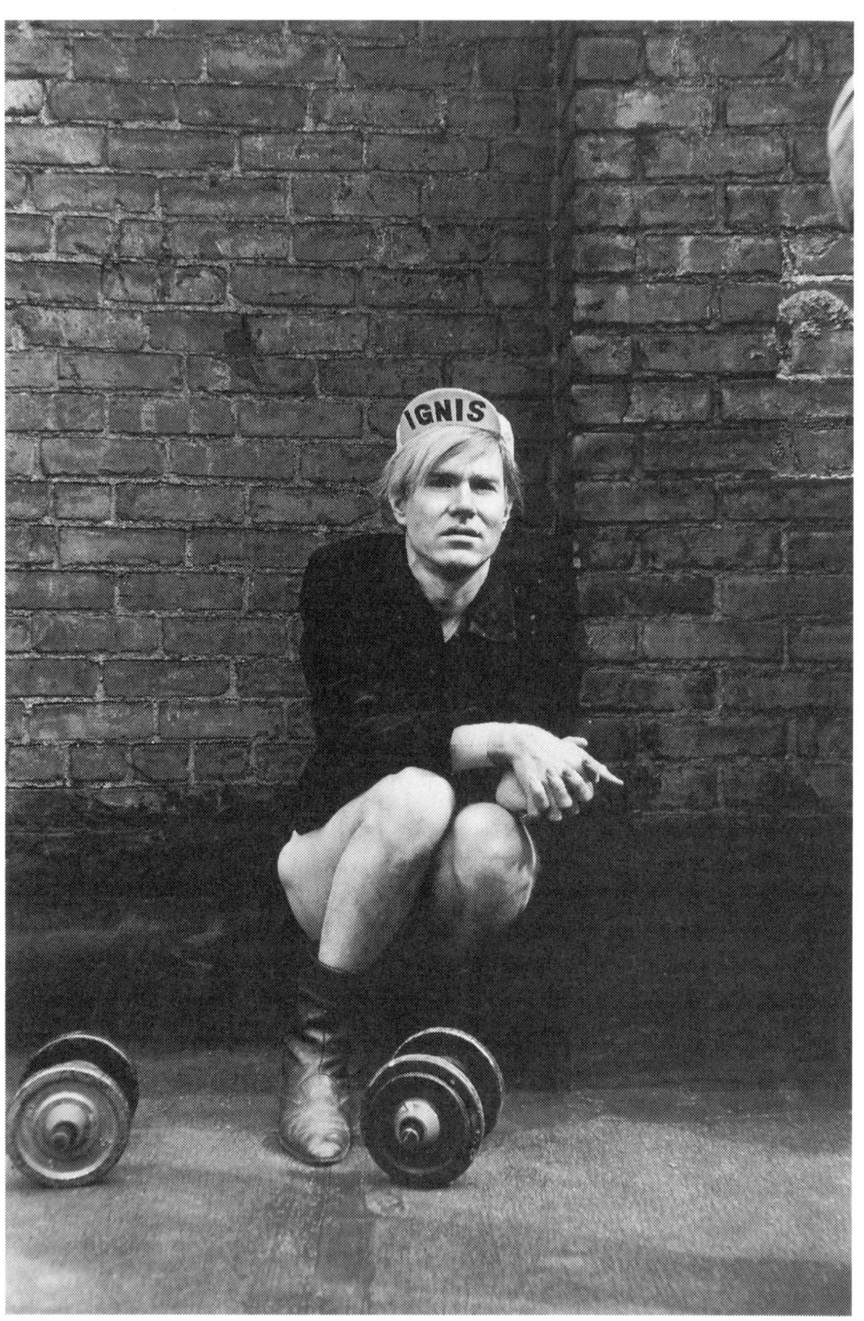

Andy Warhol in Pierro Heliczer's movie Joan of Arc, *ca. 1966. © Archives Malanga.*

filmmaking, which was a drain on him financially. Nevertheless, Edie wanted to get paid. Andy never indicated that any payment would be forthcoming, except to say to her every so often, "Be patient."

Andy assumed, wrongly perhaps, that if he paid for whatever work was involved with his projects, the result would be of poor quality. He was convinced of this. This attitude turned on him with the portrait commissions he executed during the 1970s.

At around the time Edie was losing patience with Andy, an opportunity presented itself to her. Bob Dylan's confidant and roadie, Bobby Neuwirth, acted as liaison in getting Edie to come over to the Dylan camp. The people advising Dylan thought that they could develop Edie into a singer and, in turn, capitalize on her already-established reputation in the media. So it was easy for Edie to finally leave Andy. By switching allegiance, she left the homosexual sensibility Andy represented and became part of a heterosexual milieu.

Edie's association with Dylan's group never developed in any viable way, because her talent was totally undeveloped. She thought she could further her career by being associated with Dylan, but this was merely optimism based on hope and dreams. And she soon learned that Bob had been secretly married during this time.

There are, of course, many points of view about Andy Warhol's character. A good deal of mythmaking about Andy's association with Edie has been inspired by Jean Stein and George Plimpton's book, *Edie: An American Biography*. Andy did not turn Edie on to drugs — she got caught up in the drug scene shortly after leaving him. The closest Andy ever came to taking drugs was a prescription for the diet pill Obitrol. At the time, Edie was taking Obitrols to get through the day. Andy was taking them to lose weight.

What made Andy glamorous was his unique appearance, with his silver wig and lack of pigmentation. He was instant material for the media, and deliberately became his own instant star.

Andy was also simplistic. If he said to me, "Oh, that poem was fabulous, wow!" that was the end of the discussion. But he was intelligent. He was not an impostor. On trips, many a time, we would share the same motel room, which says something about the relationship I had with him. It wasn't all that verbal, but a genuine sense of trust existed between us. This trust was simply that Andy never wanted to be alone.

Andy lived with his mother for the greater part of his adult life, up to the time she died in the late '70s. A fear of being alone was very much a part of his shyness and reticence. I don't think Andy was as much consciously trying to hide anything about himself as he was attempting to maintain a mystique to cover for his own sense of inadequacy. His shyness allowed him to be private. He felt that his sexual preferences were no one else's business, and didn't go out of his way to make a point of his homosexuality.

Many people agree that the '70s were bad years for Andy's work. In a less urgent decade than the '60s, Andy was simply out of touch with those from whom he could have benefited creatively. He relied on his fascination with the so-called rich and famous. Those people never really had anything to contribute to his art except by way of their vanity. They paid dearly for a forty-inch-square canvas of themselves. The vitality of Andy's art diminished to the point where all he was making were ooh-and-ah celebrity portraits, receiving incredible sums of money for them. I don't believe for a second that he had any genuine interest in his subjects. But these rising pop personalities that Andy had identified in his artwork of the '60s became transformed into icons for the '80s. This complete circle of events gave Andy a new surge of optimism and self-confidence... and then he died.

There's no denying that Andy Warhol is part of the history of modern art. But does the social phenomenon boost the artist or the other way around? Some claim that his greatest achievement was his adage, "In the future everyone will be famous for fifteen minutes" — a frightening thought, because the culture does seem to be developing in ways that would allow one to be famous merely on charm.

If you were to meet Andy for the first time, and he liked you, he became your instant fan, and this, in turn, would give you a feeling of importance. He had a hypnotic power to create a personality for someone. He re-created his daydreams on paper and film. The secret to Andy's success was his own self-effacement.

GERARD MALANGA's most recent book of poems is *Three Diamonds*, published by Black Sparrow Press. He divides his time between the Massachusetts Berkshires and New York City.

The Invisible Photographs

GERARD MALANGA

Dans les espaces de marées d'un corps qui se dévêt
— Paul Eluard, from "Man Ray"

What many cannot forget are her eyes.
She stands, feet planted firmly, the body
profiled on the far left of a grainy black & white photo.
Or she's standing wide-eyed behind a steamy pane of blue glass.
One hand touching the window through clouds.
The nape of a neck that rises steeply,
the tender curve of the skin behind the ear.
The hair close-cropped.
These are your attributes. These are your mysteries.
That's how Dick Avedon described you.
He said the mirror looks at you,
so the mirror looks at you.
You collect yourself.
Carefully, as if buttoning a shirt — the last button,
you compose your features.
It's a whole communion of perfumes and phrases,
of thoughts and of breathing. The eyes now averted.
The exposure double-checked: 60th at f/5.6 or eleven.
The film-speed is grainy and fast.
Rumpled tanktop.
The mauve light washing the walls.
I have never, to my mind, known anyone named Alexis Barth.

19:iii:95
Great Barrington, Mass.

Bulgaria, My Suffering

JULIA KRISTEVA

For Lydia Uldry-Natcheva

1. WHICH LANGUAGE?

I haven't forgotten my mother tongue. It comes back to me — with more and more difficulty, I admit — in dreams. Or when I hear my mother talking: then, after twenty-four hours' immersion in that now distant sea, I find I can swim in it quite well. Or again, when I'm speaking a foreign language — Russian or English, for example — if I'm at a loss for a word or can't remember the grammar, I clutch at the old lifebelt suddenly swept my way by the original source: it wasn't so deeply buried after all. So it's not French that comes to the rescue when I flounder in what amounts to an artificial code, any more than when I'm suddenly too tired to add up or multiply properly; no, the language that rises to the surface, and shows me I haven't lost touch with my beginnings, is Bulgarian.

And yet Bulgarian is already almost a dead language as far as I'm concerned. A part of me was gradually extinguished as I learned French, first with the Dominican nuns, then at the Alliance Française in Bulgaria, then at university. Lastly, exile turned the old corpus into a corpse, which it replaced with another body altogether, at first frail and artificial, then more and more indispensable; and now the sole survivor, my only living language, is French. Yet I'm almost prepared to believe in the Christian myth of resurrection when I listen, as through a stethoscope, to my own dual body and mind. For I don't definitively mourn the language of my childhood: that would imply decease, detachment, a scar, a forgetting. Instead, over that underground crypt, by that stagnant and decaying reservoir, I've built a new home: I live in it, it lives in me, and it's here that what I make bold to call *"la vraie vie,"* the true life of the mind and of the flesh, unfolds.

I feel the indescribable impact of the pearly mist that skims the Atlantic marshes, absorbing as if into swirls of Chinese silk the shrieks of the laughing gulls and the nonchalant siesta of the mallards. I dream of a spring when motor cars will be scented and poor horses will eat flowers. Apollinaire. From the vagueness which is my own immersion in being, which no swift word can sum up, for which "joy" is too ordinary and "ecstasy" too solemn, there emerges a serenity punctuated with French words. From the frontiers of my perceptions, an almost imperceptible tremor reaches out to search for the French word; from somewhere high up, at the same time but in the opposite direction, a bright mass of accumulated lava, a hoard of French reading and conversation, sends down a luminous thread that may be traced, scented out to give life to my serenity. In the alchemy of naming, I'm alone with the French language. To name being makes me be: and I live, body and soul, in French.

But whenever it comes to narrative; whenever, in other words, being presents itself as a story — a story perhaps about that pearly mist or those mallard ducks, or of course about a dream, a passion, or a murder — a great swell not made up of words, but with its own special music, forces upon me a more ungainly syntax, together with metaphors from the ocean depths which have nothing to do with French clarity and politeness, but which suffuse my serenity with Byzantine unease. And then I'm trespassing against French taste. French taste is an act of politeness between people who share the same rhetoric — the same accumulation of images and phrases, the same background of reading and conversation — within a stable society. But despite the fact that I've found new life in French — and I've been doing so for nearly fifty years now — my own French taste can't always withstand the beat of an ancient music coiled around a still-vigilant memory. My two communicating vessels bring forth a strange speech, alien to itself, belonging neither here nor there, at once foreign and intimate. Like the characters in *Le temps retrouvé* whose long years of voluntary and involuntary memory Proust sees as embodied in vast tracts of space, I am a monster of the crossroads, a freak of the forum.

At the intersection of two languages and of at least two time dimensions, I fashion a language that seeks out facts and then inserts emotional references into them, and beneath the smooth appearance of French words, as highly polished as the stone of holy-water stoups, reveals glimpses of the blackened gilt of Orthodox icons. Well, at least the resulting freak — whether giant or dwarf — is never self-satisfied, though it does annoy the natives. Those of the country I came from *and* those of the country I came to.

Whenever this anxiety — it's like an air pocket, a shortness of breath, the effects of an amphetamine — calms down enough to explain itself, I might tell you what such creatures of the frontiers are like, these unclassifiable cosmopolitans among whom I count myself. For one thing, they're the heartbeat of a modern world which, because or in spite of the pressures of immigration and interbreeding, has managed to survive its famous lost values. As a result of this, they also personify a new positive attitude that is taking shape in opposition to national conformisms and international nihilisms. More precisely, in relation to history as told by the newspapers, there are two ways of facing up to Sarajevo and the Crimea. One is to promote national languages and cultures (I'll come back to this). The other is to encourage certain species which, though still rare, are in the process of proliferating; to protect such hybrid monsters as ourselves, migrant writers who run the obvious risk of falling between two stools. Why? In order to engender new creatures of language and blood who are rooted in no one language and no one blood — diplomats of the dictionary, genetic negotiators, wandering Jews of being, who challenge all true and therefore belligerent citizens in the name of a nomadic humanity that will no longer sit still and keep quiet.

And where does suffering come in, among all these noble projects? I was expecting that question, but my answer is only half ready. There's an element of matricide in abandoning one's mother tongue, but if it has been painful for me to lose that Thracian beehive, the honey of my dreams, I've also been able to enjoy a kind of revenge, and above all take some pride in realizing an ideal first cherished by my native bees. To fly higher than one's parents did — higher, swifter, stronger! It's not for nothing that we're the heirs of the Greeks: our children will have Russian, English, French — the whole world — at their disposal. Exile, painful though it must always be, is the only way left to us, since Rabelais and the fall of the Berlin Wall, of looking for what the Fifth Book of *Pantagruel* calls the "divine bottle." This vessel is never found except by self-conscious searching, or in an exile exiling itself from the exile's certainty, the exile's arrogance. The loss is never-ending, and though a French transplant has given language and body new life, I go on listening to another pulse — that of the still-warm corpse of my maternal memory, of what I might call my mother or native memory, as one talks of one's mother or native tongue. I speak deliberately of maternal rather than involuntary or unconscious memory, because, hovering at the edge both of musical words and of inexpressible urges, near both the meaning and the biological existence my imagination is lucky enough to be able to conjure up in French, is a remembrance of suffering. Bulgaria, my suffering.

It isn't me, it's my maternal memory, a warm, still-vocal corpse, a body within my body, that throbs in time with infra-sounds and news items; with stifled loves and open conflicts; with Gregorian chant and commercial slogans; with childlike affections and awful mob violence; with political, economic, and ideological inanities; with puzzled citizens and ambitious brutes; with profiteers and slackers; with speculators in a hurry; with individualists devoid of either shame or object — and with all of you who've been left behind by history but are trying to catch up without quite knowing how; you, invisible and undesirable Bulgarians, a white blot on the light; you sombre Balkan people, transfixed by the indifference of the Western world. To which I belong. Your compliments are reproaches; your thanks are like demands; your hopes start out depressed and fall asleep before they're even expressed; your songs weep, your laughter anticipates sorrow; you're not happy, you're nonrunners. Although you set out too soon you arrive too late, in a world too old but always pretending to be younger, a world that dislikes latecomers. For some unknown reason, or none, you think the world owes you a living: you want everything, but you also want to doze, to laze, to avoid the issue, to beat about the bush and cheat, and maybe sometimes work yourselves to death, though why on earth should you? You hurt me, *mes semblables, mes frères*. Bulgaria, my suffering.

2. ERRORS OF TASTE

Let's look at it another way. If I put myself in your place, I see very clearly the arrogance of my attitude. But it is up to those who have stayed at home to deal with the reality there — in other words, as we all know, to perform the impossible. And, after all, your task isn't so very different from my own, though it operates the other way round. Your problem is to transplant into your native language (which immediately implies thoughts and lives) words (which immediately imply other thoughts and lives) from which you've been separated for fifty years by an iron curtain, and for more than a century by a democracy still in its infancy — separated, too, by an oppositional nationalism without any policy but resistance to Islam, and by a religion that ever since the Middle Ages has been faithful to its own medievalism.

I shouldn't like to be in your shoes, and I

wouldn't argue with anyone who accused me of having run away from just this problem.

They started by translating Shakespeare and Dostoevsky, then went on to Faulkner, Beckett, Nathalie Sarraute, Barthes, Foucault, Kristeva (not much of her), and others too numerous to mention. But they realized there weren't enough words available, so they crammed in — into that modest language of sensitive peasants and naïve thinkers — a whole arsenal of rootless and insipid borrowings. The syntax became unwieldy, but the thought didn't flow more freely; and what did they do but transpose this esperanto for polyglot academics into the columns of newspapers reputed to be "liberal," "cultured," and "open" to outside influence? What else can you do when nothing's any good unless it's being "opened" to outside influence? And that brings us to the inextricable confusion presented by the press since the fall of the Berlin Wall: On the one hand we have the insults of louts using the language of louts, to label as louts others equally loutish, but all completely devoid of the piquant audacity of the Surrealists; on the other hand we have the foreign words, scarcely even modified by a suffix, which dazzle a parvenu when he sees them written in Cyrillic, but, to put it mildly, arouse pity in a stateless person like me, and give a headache to what's said to be an only moderately cultured public. Thus, on one side, a flood of more or less scatological outbursts (in the name of Sade and Rabelais, let's at least have a little style!), and, on the other, the affectations of the *précieuses ridicules* (in the name of Molière and his Diafoirus, a bit of misanthropy!). On all sides, errors of taste. That is the question. Does it strike you as unimportant? Don't be in too much of a hurry. In the eighteenth century, the French talked a lot about taste. By taste they meant "the pleasures of the soul" as we experience them in *thought* and *feeling*. The Encyclopedia itself contains some celebrated articles on taste by Voltaire and Montesquieu, who reflected on the universal laws governing its formation (based on the universality of human nature and on a shared history), and on the permissibility of individual lapses or *departures* from the norm. The Encyclopedists were bound to take a new stance: taste, for them, is a rhetoric of recognition. It is necessary that *I* recognize myself, that *you* recognize yourself, and that we recognize ourselves either in some authority (Church or monarchy, preferably both); or in an elite taken to represent the essence of that authority (the court at Versailles); or in some individual value, derived from Christianity, that manifests itself in the form of extreme spirituality or intense passion (Universal Reason or enlightened sensuality). Taste is the rhetoric of a recognition by which the ego, centred on Authority, the clan, or an individual hypostasis, finds in the other the same language as he finds in himself. Taste can accommodate difference between the ego and the other if, and only if, that difference blends — and for me harmony is like a pleasant flavour — with the relevant Authority, clan, or individual, whereupon the two principles share the same language.

Taste is polite because it is addressed to one's own kind: those who share the same authority, the same clan, the same personal values. La Bruyère, Sévigné, and Saint-Simon didn't need to define taste — it went without saying. But the Encyclopedists, testing to destruction the standards of the *Ancien Régime*, considered the possibility of a new kind of taste, one that admitted the notion of liberty and even allowed for the aberration of passion. These prerevolutionaries were among the most civilized people the West has ever known. Nearer to our own day, Proust, after losing his footing in the baptistery at St. Mark's and stumbling in the Guermantes' courtyard, set himself up as the explorer of errors of taste, laughing at the whole concept for the sake of literature, the only authority that still seemed capable of preserving it.

But things are different now, when barbarism is crumbling and the Mafia vies with free enterprise. There is no authority, and neither community nor the individual exists. In the absence of these three references, the intellectual, who, when all is said and done, is a creator of language, is inevitably left liable to errors of taste. And no one now, like Proust, believes in literature enough to laugh at this state of affairs and press on. No one, or very few.

I'd like to stress this apparently minor point. I might have lamented the exorbitant prices prevailing in the black market; the miserly old-age pensions; the dustbins and flies in once-so-clean Sofia; the merging of socialists with liberals, and vice versa, which blurs everything and makes all decision impossible. But I'd rather concentrate on taste. If we begin with small things, we'll meet with larger ones on our way.

I'm not at all sure that if I were in your position I'd have been able to discover some authority, community, or person, and consequently some kind of taste. But I certainly would have tried to avoid words that didn't emanate from the authority of a group, or from the charisma of an individual courteous enough to seek recognition from others concerned with the same politeness. Without that concern, words are no more than odd foreign neologisms stuck at random in sand not quick but dead — snobbish nonsense; high-sounding foolishness. Without politeness, they're an affront. Such errors of taste reveal the barbarity of a whole society.

"Другостта фалическия ДИСКУРС," or more simply, "той се грижи за своя имидж," or much more ponderously: "Освен това, знаейки твърде добре историята на революциите, тъжната истина, че те изяждат своите деца, демократичните избори би трябвало да бъдат известна ПРЕВЕНЦИЯ, средство за спиране на революцията с нашето участие в тях прекъсване на ужасяващата връзка с историческия революционен опит" — this sort of thing makes me feel sick. I won't suggest alternatives, although *дискурс* is the same thing as *реч*, *имидж* means *образ*, *представа*, or *картина*, and *превенция* might be rendered as *възпрепятствие*, and *пречка* as *предпазна мярка*.

Stop it! Please! Invent words if you like, but not words empty of the ideas you lack. Cut out sentences based on foreign syntax, expressing thoughts you don't understand. Change your tune: stop mumbling the old rudimentary simplicities, but don't try to imitate the tricks of those who belong to a baroque, sophisticated culture which you know nothing about. Don't imitate other people at all: they're just as difficult and unstable as you are. Have confidence in yourself: no graft will ever take on too weak a stock.

In theory I'm not against neologisms, so long as they arise from an attempt at new thinking; so long as communities of men and women have shaped them carefully to produce something unique, based on the memory of their own language and on suitable discussion. But I can't see any of these communities or inventions; I can't see this linguistic memory or these debates. That's what makes me suffer. Perhaps it's only blindness; perhaps, being so far away, I don't know what's really going on. That would be a lesser evil, and if such is the case I apologize. But if my suffering is justified, the errors of taste that cause it are conclusive proof of the surrender and submission of a nation (one of many) to a new world order that would like to see the whole human race as a single person. What am I saying? As a single computer.

3. WHEN DID GOD DIE FOR THE BALKANS?

You suffer from chaos, vandalism, violence. You suffer from lack of authority. You suffer from corruption, from lack of initiative, from general indifference combined with unprecedented individual brutality, from the arrogance of the Mafia and the shady schemes of the nouveaux riches.

It's hard for the West to imagine your suffering, your humiliation. I hesitate to say I share them: it's too easy to do that from a distance. But let's say I do suffer because of the enormous task that faces us all, whether here or there, in the coming years: the task of thinking, why? Why is everything like this? And then the task of finding out how to put it behind us.

Needless to say, I don't know the answer. Nor will I repeat what you know already about the responsibility of Communism or the shortcomings of democracy in Bulgaria's early days: ever since its liberation from the Turks in 1875, it has suffered from the repercussions of European diplomacy and the effects of two world wars. On a more personal level, and since I'm talking about language, there's the question of mental attitudes. And I, like many other observers, note that the moral crisis afflicting the former Communist bloc seems more hopeless, with fewer short-term prospects and perhaps a more barbaric side to it, in countries that profess the Orthodox faith. Of this kind of disaster, Serbian neofascism is a supreme example. And it makes me ponder.

I don't believe there is such a thing as an overall "popular psychology." I believe in the uniqueness of the individual. Nor do I hold religion alone responsible for the way people behave. I know it's of relatively little importance in areas steeped in folklore and paganism, and this is especially true of contemporary generations. Even so, a person's religious outlook, shaped by and in turn shaping history, does, *among other factors*, affect him or her, whether consciously or not. It also exerts a major influence on the psychological buck which the peoples of the Europe we hope to unite pass back and forth between them, in the form of conflicts manifesting themselves at worst as wars of religion and at best as stubborn incomprehension and incompatibility.

Thanks to my father, I was able to encounter the Orthodox faith and experience its latent power of resistance. I love its sensuality, its mystery, and the remoteness that makes us sense in its liturgy the joys and sorrows of another world. It also imbues us with the feeling — it's not a rational certainty — that we are not really of this world. True, it's only an impression, perhaps an illusion, but how happy, how liberating and auspicious! I won't make a value judgment and praise the "virtues" of one branch of Christianity as against the "shortcomings" of another. I'll simply try to tell you how I see the advantages and limitations of someone conditioned by Orthodoxy, and to examine the extent of his or her ability to confront the moral crisis.

Even before the schism of 1054, the Orthodox branch of Christianity harboured two tendencies which have been growing more marked ever since, and which are reflected in the various national churches (Russian, Greek, Bulgarian, and so on). The two tendencies I refer to are instrumentalisation and mysticism.

By instrumentalisation I mean, first of all, the Church's dependence on political power, a dependence which has often degenerated into self-effacement or even outright subservience. This derives from the Byzantine principle according to which a patriarch holds his territory by virtue of a *secular* act determined by the prevailing political climate (whereas Rome claimed to rule by *divine* law): the basileus or Byzantine emperor intervenes in the affairs of the Church and chooses the patriarch, and in return the Church works to maintain social stability and religious conservatism. "For a Christian there can be no church without an emperor": this dictum of the patriarch Anthony (1391–1397) has a sinister ring when one thinks of the political allegiances the Orthodox churches have entered into and the acts of servility they have performed in the twentieth century. This situation culminates in an identification of the Church with the nation which in the Middle Ages produced the young Slav states (as seen in the lives of Boris and Simeon and the invention of the Cyrillic alphabet), and now is responsible for the current *strange osmosis between religion and nationalism.* The reductive and explosive effects of this mixture may well have been underestimated by historians appraising the "liberating role" played by the churches against the Turkish occupation in the nineteenth century; the same effects, with all their fundamentalist dangers, can be seen all too clearly in the tragedy of Yugoslavia today.

By instrumentalisation I also mean certain aspects of the Orthodox Trinity. *God* is triple in Orthodox Christianity as in Catholicism, but in a different way: for Orthodox believers, the Holy Ghost proceeds from the Father *through* the Son *(Per Filium)*; for Catholics, from the Father *and* the Son *(Filioque)*. While the Catholic "and" puts Father and Son on a footing of equality, foreshadowing the autonomy and independence of the individual (that of the Son just as much as that of the believer, which opens the way to Western individualism and personalism), the Orthodox "through" suggests a pleasurable but pernicious annihilation.

The omnipotent authority of the Father is inalienable: the Father, *arkè-anarkos,* is both deity and source. The Son is his servant, a colleague who rises above his servitude ("through") and becomes divine. At once subordinate and godlike, the Son (and the believer with him) is caught up in an exquisite logic of submission and exaltation offering the joys and sorrows involved in the master-slave dialectic and, on a more personal plane, in male homosexuality.

Moreover, as a result of the exalted and exalting subordination of the Son, religion descends from the superior sublunary world where Platonism located God to become a *human* and *social* programme. Russian theologians have not shrunk from stressing the humanistic "advantages" of Orthodoxy: through its doctrine of the Trinity and the *collaborative* role of the Son, Orthodoxy celebrates a "God-humanity" or a "God-universe" (Solovyov); some commentators even go so far as to say that "the Trinity is our social programme" (Fyodorov).

But we mustn't rejoice too soon at this humanization of the divine. If it's true that human values are corruptible and subject to perversion, doesn't the reduction of the supreme value (God) to human value represent the ultimate trap of nihilism? For the *instrumentalisation of the divine in the human* results in the lowering, devaluation, and even abolition of the ideal itself — of God himself (God is neither this nor that, neither affirmation nor negation, nor even "God," according to Gregory of Palamas); of spiritual authority (except that which is institutional); and also of the *eidos*, the idea, itself, and so of representation, of thought. The Orthodox religion is a negative theology from the outset: it treats absence of God and the unknowable as the same. God is not dead — he implodes into man, an inaccessible microtheos and microcosm.

This reduction of the divine to the human is counterbalanced by *mysticism*. Man, who at once collaborates with God and lowers Him, makes himself divine by attaining direct access to the unfathomable: Orthodox man is a "Homo absconditus," indefinable, impossible to conceptualise. This mystery has produced endless delights. There is, for example, the cult of *silence*: spiritual excellence is silent (as was shown by the *hesychasts*, the quietists of Mount Athos); the cult of affection *(katanyxis)*, which welcomes but does not judge. There is also the unification of conscience and heart in the *love of beauty (Philocallie)*. Living divinity, like a sea of light, manifests itself in *gentleness*, yielding itself not to argument but to heart or feeling. Isaac of Syria's "feeling of everything in God" becomes a cult of the "feeling of God," rejecting *words* and departing from the logical path of Catholic and Protestant theology. *Apophasis* is the culminating point of this *negative theology*, which denies all conceptual definition of God. Neither value nor concept nor representation, God is the inaccessible participator and participated, the unfathomable mystery, the unobjectivisable.

Because of the obvious benefits of this kind of religious experience, I run the risk of promoting *the strongest form of nihilism* known to Western culture. "I am God who is not so." The meeting point of the absolute and nothingness. The desire for total power and total poverty. These juxtapositions might challenge Western onto-theology. They might, in certain historical and philosophical circumstances, act as a salutary counterpart to it. It's easy to see why Heidegger succumbed to the charms of the monks of Mount Athos. But Orthodoxy does not invalidate onto-theology: it merely skirts around it and immobilizes its agents.

On the one hand, Orthodoxy, caught in a pincer movement between instrumentalisation and mysticism, provides the paranoid and masochistic satisfactions that Dostoevsky has shown in his nihilistic characters, especially Raskolnikov. The Orthodox Trinity's "unmoving motion of love" (as Maxim the Confessor called it) cannot encounter history except through action: individual terrorism shatters the contemplation in which our "microtheos" delights, while state terrorism compensates for inability to verbalize and lack of education and opportunity.

On the other hand, the symbiosis of the Trinity in Orthodoxy makes Nietzsche's "God is dead" impossible. How can He be dead, when "I" am He, and He has vanished into "me"? While to proclaim "God is dead" is probably crazy as an idea, it is certainly dangerous and perhaps impossible as an act; yet it has preoccupied the West, stealthily, ever since its Greek, biblical, and evangelical origins, more openly since the nineteenth century. The phrase itself addresses the Ideal, the possibility that man may have Values; but it is also implied in Europe's Catholic and Protestant past. The philosophers, from Nietzsche to Heidegger, who have studied the current crisis have envisaged a *transmutation of values* carried out via the autonomous Subject. *But not an abolition of values altogether.*

Protestantism was a response to a phase of this crisis that occurred in the sixteenth century, but it derived from the rationalism of the West as a whole, and saw *predestination* as a kind of unease urging Protestant man towards asceticism, methodical labour, professional success, and scientific research. All these were signs of election, pressed into service by rising capitalism. The Protestant ethic, even in its narrowest Puritan version, was a result of individual autonomy, and it was often based on rejection of the mystery of the Trinity. It is an improvement on, not an attempt to destroy, the urge towards the Ideal (or God). The secular, Masonic, and esoteric surrogates of Protestantism are based on the preservation of Value, and are vehemently against any attempt to abolish it.

The Nietzschean revolt followed a completely different path: it aimed at examining the sources of the Ideal and its underlying strata of will, desire, and power in order to reveal other possible relationships between Being and man. The "superman," it should be stressed, is by no means a "public layabout"; he is, rather, a "subversion" of man, a rebel excavating the archaeology of his own essence.

Orthodox man — instrumentalised and mystical — cannot measure up to these two representatives of modernity. He lacks the ascetic autonomy, the hardworking sobriety, the bookish virtue of the Protestant, seeking salvation in the written word (the Bible) and in the city (the spirit of enterprise). He also lacks the philosophical distance of the fanatical Nietzschean, dissociating himself from God and spending nearly three centuries refining the emblems of the *Ego Cogito* in order to envisage different relationships with original Being, knowledge, and pleasure.

We of the Orthodox tradition are heirs to a victorious nihilism. But delightful as that may be, it leaves us defenceless in the face of contemporary history, if indeed it doesn't turn us into "public layabouts." For two thousand years, values have been imploding in us, and we at once lament and enjoy this immanentized, cancelled-out, transcendence. We have placed ourselves outside history — an act of excessive virtue. But history goes on, and after the digression of Communism — which was in a way a piece of luck, though a costly one, because it spared us the necessity of questioning ourselves — history now calls to us. But do we really want to rejoin it? As nihilists, we feel we have been "had." That is the cause of my suffering, and I can't see any way out. Bulgaria, my suffering.

Don't think I'm not serious, and don't say I've said what I haven't said. No. It's too late — no point in your converting to Catholicism or even to Protestantism. Just the same, let's face up to the awful truth that in the world of advanced capitalism which you'd like to join, God is dead. And let's try neither to ignore nor to exploit this world. Let's neither hurl ourselves greedily on its untenable values nor decry them. Rather let us take part in their transmutation.

We might begin with quite simple things. By setting ourselves to read, for example, to decipher texts — the Greeks, the Bible, the Gospels, the philosophers, writers in general. To comment, discuss, understand. We might also examine ourselves: look after our own autonomy, desires, and dignity; have ourselves psychoanalyzed, take a course of psychotherapy. Try out some religious experiences, the asceticism of the Protestants, the pleasure of the Catholics — why not others, too? Or go back to Orthodoxy, escape from its snares, make its demands for community more concrete and more effective. Rediscover a sense of values; express them, transform them, leave them open, never stop renovating them... It's going to take a long, long time. Bulgaria, my suffering.

My attention has been called to a well-known text by Thomas Mann: a journal he kept during the Nazi regime, when he was living in exile. It's called "Germany, My Suffering." Mann sees the tragedy of his country from both within and without, and while he condemns the shame of Hitlerism he is also aware of the furtive complicity the majority of Germans felt for the man they didn't hesitate to call their "brother Hitler." The violence and barbarity of the Third Reich has nothing in common with the collapse of morals and politics in the former Communist Empire — a collapse with which the Western democracies, shaken by so many scandals, are not unfamiliar, though their crisis is on a much smaller scale. So there is no direct link between Thomas Mann's journal and my own notes. Except perhaps that both texts are written from a position at once within and without, and both express anxiety at an upheaval whose ravages hit us plainly and head-on, but whose consequences remain hidden in the future.

Translated from the French by Barbara Bray

JULIA KRISTEVA is professor at the Université de Paris VII. An internationally known psychoanalyst and critic, she is the chief proponent of "semanalyse," a term she coined to name the discipline blending semiotics with psychoanalysis. Her many book include *Black Sun, Strangers to Ourselves,* and *New Maladies of the Soul.* BARBARA BRAY was born in London and educated at Cambridge University. She has lived for the past thirty years in Paris as a freelance writer, critic, and translator.

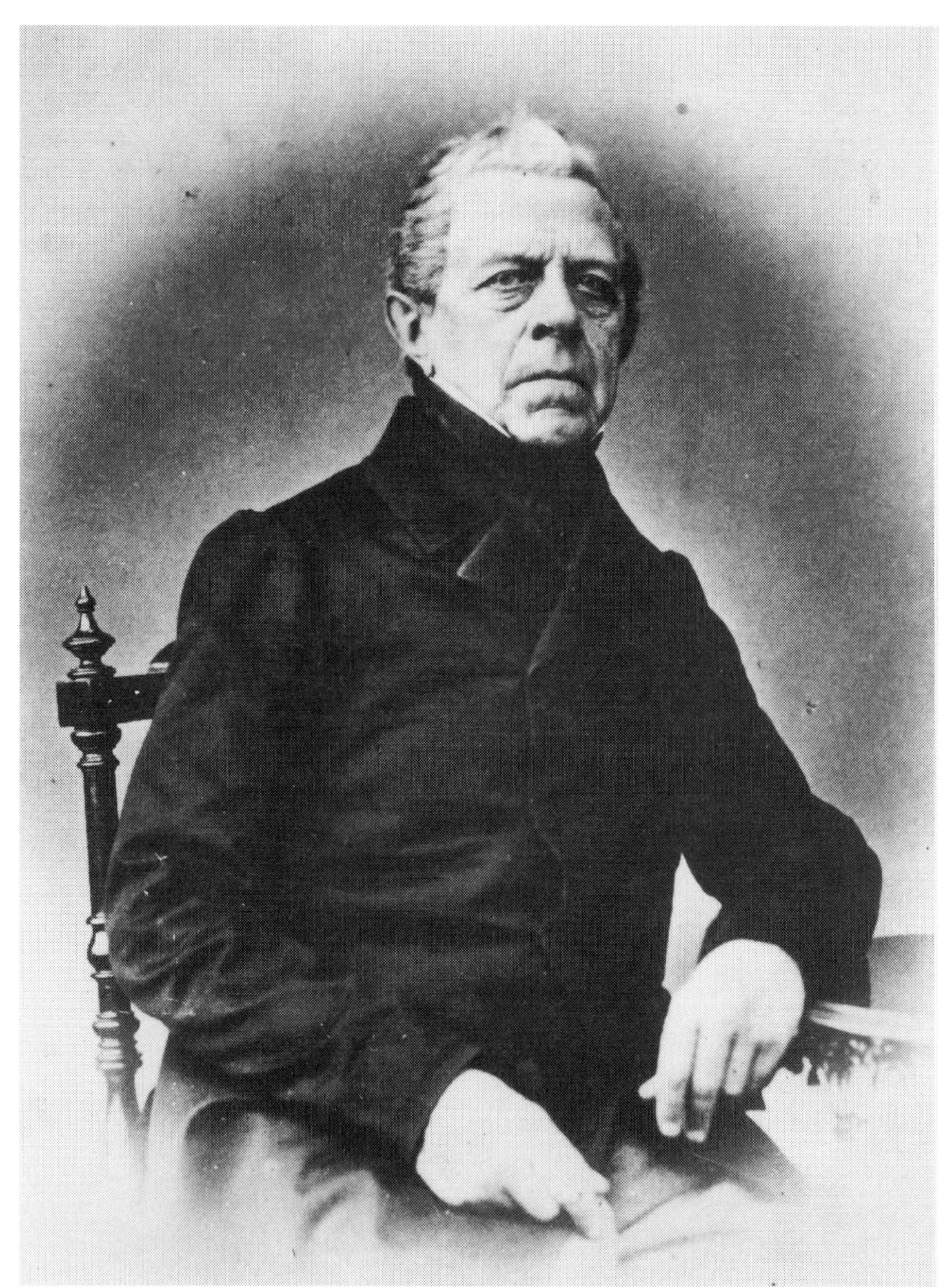

Franz Berwald, 1862.

The Private Life of Mr. Franz Berwald

ALF THOOR

It was a very long time ago.

The way I remember the 150th anniversary of Berwald's birth, in 1946, it was part of a sort of Scandinavian musical championships. The heavyweight class.

Sweden's situation was disquieting.

Norway, Denmark, and Finland all had their big guns.

Grieg, born in 1843, died in 1907, belonged among the minor classics and was known the world over: the piano concerto, the music for *Peer Gynt,* and "Solveig's Song," which some Swede or other was always having played for him by an attentive violinist in a restaurant in Canberra, where they thought that Sweden was the capital of Oslo.

Carl Nielsen, born in 1865, died in 1931, was regarded in Sweden right up to the 1940s as a leading international modernist, even by the youngest generation, who towards the end of World War II had flung themselves into the wild storm of the avant-garde.

Sibelius, born in 1865 and still alive at eighty-one, was reckoned in Britain and the United States to be among the century's giants, and rumours of an Eighth Symphony came and went at that time and were not denied.

But Sweden, what did Sweden have?

The correct answer would be: Franz Berwald.

Born in 1796, he was therefore a year older than Schubert and a decade older than the classical Romantics whose approach he shared: Schumann, Mendelssohn. He died in 1868, a year before Berlioz, another contemporary he is sometimes — with more or less justification — compared to.

Swedish commentators in that first postwar period boldly placed him among the nineteenth century's symphonic explorers, one of those who genuinely went their own way. At the same time, this provided a natural explanation of the fact that he was so overlooked. But now it was time to catch up with him and make his music ours in the international orchestra.

Easier said than done.

The neighbouring countries gave a friendly if sceptical nod and allotted him his quota in line with the exchange rates. International performances occurred on a random basis, often, perhaps, on the initiative of conductors wishing to obtain engagements in Sweden. In this area a type of diplomacy is practised whose aims are not always what they appear to be.

In foreign handbooks and dictionaries of music, Berwald was alternately included and omitted. The Germans, moreover, true to form, preferred to call him "Swedish composer of German extraction." And the fact was undeniable:

his father came to Sweden in the 1770s in connection with Gustavus III's cultural expansion and sat in the Royal Opera House Orchestra as a violinist until 1806. To that extent, the lustre of future triumphs was undeniably tarnished, viewed from just this nationalistic perspective: in the same degree to which one tried to make Berwald stand out as a significant, independent innovator, German opinion-makers tried to Germanize him.

It was a whole cultural syndrome we were confronted with, a cluster of syndromes, sensitivities, and traumatic experience, and we still couldn't even give it its proper name. Because of our hazy national identity we wished for a classical symphonist, but the tradition he held in trust in his symphonies stretched from, roughly, Haydn to Bruckner.

This was the international perspective we were so keen to be part of. But Swedish melodies from Berwald's time sounded more like provincial folksongs. It is true that researchers knew a Berwald who was on that level of complexity too, the Berwald of the royal anthems, of the operetta *The Milliner's Assistant,* the patriotic cantatas, all this home-grown Swedish music which is like an outstretched hand — listen to me! understand me! But that dilemma was largely a question of social contacts, and to some extent bread-and-butter stuff.

Certainly, someone who feels he has important things to communicate can also somehow convince himself that the first priority is to make people listen. And then ...!

When Berwald cobbled together music for his few Swedish concerts, a grim truth was brought home to him. If there existed — in little, out-of-the-way Stockholm — any general, common experiences to connect with, they were either local or antiquated. This was the original one-horsetown. Coteries ruled. There were certainly people who knew what was going on down there on the Continent, for this was also the time of the radical and freethinking writer Jonas Love Almqvist, but their concerns were not Berwald's concerns. His radicalism had to do with music and almost nothing else.

After thirteen years on the Continent, in Berlin and Vienna, he presents himself in Stockholm in 1842, forty-six years old, with a programme that could not have been more ambitious: "a great Musical Academy." The Royal Opera House Orchestra plays under the conductor himself, Franz Berwald's cousin Johan Fredrik (which does not appear to have given him any advantages). Out of ten pieces played, eight are by Franz Berwald himself.

He must have planned to take his rightful place in the musical life of Stockholm — at last! It didn't happen that way. The public went on strike. The venue, a large church, is described as almost empty, the atmosphere was low-key, the acoustics deplorable, the reviews pitying.

The next few years can be viewed as a struggle against superior forces. He is strong, but the opposition is stronger. How Berwald supports himself and his young wife is unclear — the odd concert brings in money, and no doubt he also gives lessons, but too much of his life is taken up with this. He despises lucre, he says, but most of the time he manages to ensure that he has some, and as soon as he does, he shares it with his sisters: a practical fellow, and a comfort and support to his nearest and dearest. He has an air of bourgeois solidity.

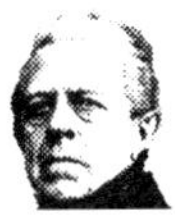

Look at his face! He wasn't one to give in, that much is clear. Everything he takes up bespeaks his stubbornness and defiant energy, to say nothing of the contrapuntal interplay of all the different states of mind — generosity, astringent humour, rigorous objectivity, lyricism, tenderness, wild exhilaration. His emotional states vary, but the dourness endures. His portraits confirm details gleaned from anecdotes about him, and from his music. There is a harmony between picture, word, and sound which compensates for many a gap in the biographical material.

The play between the external and the internal in the music is, to be sure, an elusive phenomenology, but look at Berwald's face, and at the same time listen to a slow movement in one of his symphonies! That crusty fellow! Yet at the same time, the loving, deep-rooted tenderness of the melody!

That sort of duplicity is hard to take for those around one; this much must be said in defence of Franz Berwald's recalcitrant countrymen. One shouldn't demand too much. People whose competence is rejected and whose motives are questioned are not likely to rejoice at their rival's genius. That his heart was in the right place is the kind of thing people tend to say afterwards.

The human comedy doesn't alter. The more it changes, the more it stays the same. But as far as the history of Swedish music is concerned, the years 1842–46 are a tragedy. A tremendous opportunity is lost. Music lies in readiness, waiting to be performed, shimmering life slumbers between closed covers bearing titles like *Sinfonie sérieuse, Sinfonie singulière*. Before it can be presented in a Swedish setting, and even begin to put down roots, thirty, fifty, sixty years have passed, or perhaps even longer, for root systems do not so easily allow themselves to be uncovered.

Perhaps the most original work that Berwald ever wrote, the Symphony in F Major (the "Singular"), dated March 1845, was performed for the first time in January 1905.

So what is "our time"? Which Sweden is Berwald's Sweden?

Another chronology is discernible, located in layers of time and structures that can only exist in our imagination, in our experience.

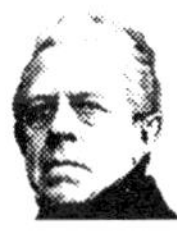

For anyone wishing to examine the implications of the expression "to be ahead of one's time," few examples can be more illustrative than that of Franz Berwald in Sweden during the 1840s.

To be in tune with one's time is something else. There, too, Berwald's case merits study. For instance, there is a "Fantasy Piece" dated 4th July, 1844, the day of Oscar I's coronation, and entitled "King Oscar!" — exclamationmark and all — "And Dedicated to All the Friends of Song, BY FRANZ BERWALD." As far as the lyrics are concerned, the opening words will suffice:

"Svea, mother of heroes, sat..."

The prodigal son seems to have been trying to announce that he was home again. It looks as if he were prepared to do what was expected of him.

The symphonies lay in his writing desk. It is almost impossible to grasp: mute.

But just look at his face!

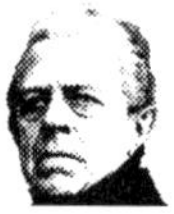

The relationship between society and music is as complicated as that between society and language: a seamless, confused interaction in which the observer has to learn himself by heart — his experience, his expectations — and try to see how the future is anticipated in the present. Now, in the 1990s, when so many hopes for the future of the world have been crushed, one might ask oneself to what extent the sociologist's assessment of trends differs from a Rorschach test. If countless prophets prophesy, perhaps he is a great prophet who happens to guess right. For who can be bothered to worry about the others, however magnificent their visions may have been?

The relationship between Sweden and Franz Berwald was not only complicated, it was also downright abrasive: communication of a very low-key variety. The reasons for his leaving the country in 1829 — rather late in life; he was already thirty-three years old — need not have been so very remarkable. He wanted to get away. But this self-assured man must certainly have been tired of the way the press constantly treated him like an industrious apprentice who might possibly amount to something, though perhaps not yet.

The Stockholm Opera and the Royal Opera House Orchestra had, to be sure, a new lease on life under the Swiss-Frenchman Edouard Du Puy, who was also Berwald's teacher. A school for string-players had been set up. We know the names of several first-class instrumentalists, like, for example, the Finnish Swede Bernhard Crusell, one of the best clarinettists of his day. But by now Berwald had spent sixteen years among the first violins in the Royal Opera House Orchestra. He must have known that he would find no more musical stimulation in that land gone astray; Sweden was still fully occupied with the re-conquest of Finland, but now within Sweden's own borders — a classic formulation by the national bard Esaias Tegnér for constructing a new identity.

Now he is a composer, nothing else. In olden days, they would have said he was seeking his fortune, that he wanted quite simply to conquer the world. By virtue of the odd piece of music, we can infer that by this time he had a superb knack with the composing pen. The question of where he had learnt, and from whom, is not necessarily crucial.

From the year 1828, there is a septet for string quartet and three wind-players (including clarinet — one can picture Crusell in the roulades), which on a good day can lift the roof off any modern concert-palace. I have had it as a companion myself over the years, and have always marvelled at its effervescence, extravagance, and pace. Berwald plays, like a circus juggler, with the classical forms, and strikes up a sinfonietta for seven instruments. You could alternate it with Prokofiev's *Classical Symphony*: a greeting from the one century to the other.

In the culture of more musical countries, successful masterpieces like this have become hits that bring a sparkle to people's eyes. But for Berwald the doors did not open. The fairy tale of the ugly duckling was not about him. He had to pack his trunk and head for Berlin, and there is not the slightest indication that anyone tried to talk him into coming home again.

On the contrary, many people must have been delighted that he stayed away. Look at his face!

To fall out with this man would not have been a good idea.

For thirteen years, they were rid of him.

II.

It is gradually dawning on me that I am writing this in a spirit of being wise after the event.

We wiseacres ought to know better — if not in earlier times, then now, in the 1990s. We have witnessed the aberrations of the Zeitgeist and the collapse of the science of prognostication. Kremlinologists, where are you now? Political economists, whatever happened to Reaganomics? And the Laffer curve?

Bearing in mind the Berwald commemoration of 1946, it also feels unfair to moralize solely about the little Sweden of Carl XIV Johan.

One hundred and fifty years after Berwald's birth, those of us who were concerned with what in the language of the day was called "serious music" thought that the time had come. The plinth was there. The monument could be put in place.

I remember it well, for it so happened that I wrote my first review for a daily newspaper just after the jubilee concert. I was drafted at the last minute, because the regular music critic had absconded to Switzerland for a conference on ethics. The paper's circulation was only 31,000, but the pressure on the reviewer was close to unbearable: deadline, 12:30 a.m., copy snatched from the writer's hand at 12:37. To keep tabs on such an event was a matter of prestige for a little paper with serious pretensions.

History weighed heavily on these solemnities. Speeches were made about the great inheritance that was ours to administer. Flowers were laid on the grave. The ceremonial side of things was taken care of, with tailcoats and literary prose, by the Academy of Music itself and the concert societies.

Yet, in the end, the celebrations concluded rather strangely: a passing affair, and of relevance only to an intimate inner circle.

The values of the Establishment at large were better expressed by the post office. At that time, they had a parsimonious attitude towards new stamp issues, so the question of the special stamp for the year was to some extent a matter of public concern. The newspapers debated the issue, and possibly even the radio, which otherwise would have stayed neutral. Interested parties put their word in, including those in the music world. Surely this was the right year for Berwald?

The post office didn't think so. A communiqué announced that the theme of that year's stamp would be the Fourth Farmers' Congress. So it transpired, and it came out on the right day, the 4th of July, with a calf on it.

Franz Berwald emigrated twice in his lifetime. Something tells me that Swedish society would have been prepared to let the composer emigrate yet again if anyone had begun to make demands on the recalcitrant Berwald's behalf. The 150th-anniversary commemoration mattered only to those with a specialist interest and was not something which, for symbolic significance, could be compared to the Fourth Farmers' Congress.

As I write, a scene occurs to me. There were a group of us who, on this occasion, back in the 1950s, paid a call on our worthy finance minister. It was about money for a gramophone project. We wanted to bring out some older Swedish music, including Berwald, on records, and we speechified in fine style about documentation, about hidden treasures waiting to be rediscovered, about the new technology that was creating new forms of communication and altering our picture of the present and the past.

The finance minister was not sympathetic.

"So many people come asking for money," he said. "I've just had some representatives from the horse-racing industry here."

III.

Relationships have their beginning and their continuation, and perhaps a basic quality which is preserved. There is something familiar about the very earliest evidence regarding Berwald's relations with his surroundings, both near and far.

He has his own compositions performed around 1820, and soon there are complaints from people who stand up for "generally valid rules." They are following with unease the course of development after Haydn and Mozart. Beethoven meets with their approval, but only for the works of his youth. Afterwards he went astray, they think nervously. The choral finale in the Ninth Symphony sounds — according to one notorious review — like a band of wild Tierra del Fuegans, shrieking and whooping as they devour their diet of raw fish.

Now this Berwald is heading in the same direction. "Chasing after originality and striving to impress merely by means of grand effects," he has "assiduously banished from his compositions all that is melodious; for how can one otherwise explain these eternal modulations from one key to another, which made such an odious impression and failed to grant the attention some resting-place."

The anonymous writer in the journal *Argus* was indignant: "As soon as a melody made itself heard, it was immediately broken off, and the ear was tormented incessantly with the most painful dissonances, which at length became almost totally unbearable. It might also be salutary for a composer to remember that harmony must always be subservient to melody: that the former exists only for the sake of the latter."

Berwald was not at a loss for an answer. For the first, but certainly not the last time, he became involved in a public controversy.

It is without the least surprise that he reads the review in *Argus*, we learn. But the reviewer can rest assured that Berwald "...had myself foreseen the rather unfavourable impression that these works, written in a completely original style, would make." For "... all attempts [at composition] based on a less than usual system, a newer form of orchestration and its application would always initially meet with numerous difficulties."

And as for the reviewer's assertion that "... my subjects were not properly developed": "... what a gross error! If the Reviewer would merely take the trouble to acquire the relevant facts from the score, insofar as he is capable of judging such things — which I greatly doubt — then I would hope easily to convince him of the contrary."

That is self-esteem. That is conviction: this I have done, this I stand by. Berwald writes of his "systemic change" in a way that brings both Wagner and Schönberg to mind; leaving aside other comparisons.

Look at his face!

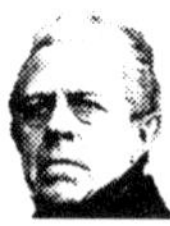

We must bear in mind that this approach to music was the mirror image of his approach to human beings. When it came to cultivating human contacts, Berwald could be his own worst enemy. He stuck to his guns. He didn't keep his thoughts to himself. In this way, he made many friends and many enemies.

There is an episode which shows how he created problems for himself and how, perhaps, the course of history was influenced by his rigidity — and how, in that way, Berwald became Berwald.

On the 26th of May, 1829, he travels south.

"Oddly enough," he writes in a letter, "at the age of 33 my father journeyed from Germany to Sweden, and at the same age and almost the same time of year I travelled from Sweden to Germany."

It turned out well for him; he searched out some well-off relatives and was helped to find his footing by people of influence, Swedes and others. He came into contact with the Mendelssohn family, even receiving a Christmas present from them, and of course met Felix.

The meeting was not a success. Felix Mendelssohn was now an inordinately celebrated twenty-year-old; in that very year of 1829, he had resurrected Bach's *St. Matthew Passion,* and the whole music world knew who he was. This was evident in his home. "The family built a ring around him," noted one who had been there.

In April 1830, Felix Mendelssohn writes a letter to his close friend, the Swedish composer Adolf Fredrik Lindblad, and complains about this Berwald. One cannot like him. He fusses, and boasts, and is pompous. He says that Weber, Spohr, and Spontini are bunglers, and talks of wretched elements in Beethoven's *Fidelio.* Mendelssohn thinks that Berwald is an oaf who has nothing of interest to offer apart from echoes of Swedish folksongs.

The urbane Felix Mendelssohn was angry. He expected, of course, to be greeted more courteously. But Berwald was thirty-three years old, after all, and perhaps thought he was talking to a boy wonder who could benefit from learning this and that. I imagine him saying from time to time, like so many other well-read and domineering characters, "I'm not boasting, I'm just stating how things are."

With the support of the Mendelssohn family, he could have had another fate in store for him in Berlin. Now, he was beating his head against a brick wall. Success, he believed, meant having something performed at the Opera. So he searched for subjects and librettists and launched one opera project after another into slow oblivion. He managed to struggle along.

By 1835, every possibility seems to have been exhausted. Then an unforeseen quality of Berwald's manifests itself. Previously, he has staked everything on his career as a composer, but now he turns a somersault and starts up an orthopaedic institute based on sound ideas borrowed from Pehr Henrik Ling, the "father of Swedish gymnastics." And here, suddenly, Berwald struck it lucky. Gymnastics and exercise were in fashion, and the fact that his methods came from the barren, snowy north was no disadvantage.

What was in his mind, we do not know. He seems to have done his composing in the mornings. And with furious energy, we may imagine, for a few years later he returns to Sweden as a mature symphonist, becoming, in time, a nineteenth-century Swedish Charles Ives, torn between his managerial post and musical creativity.

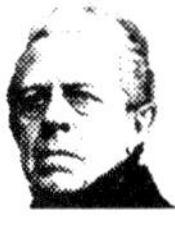

In 1841, he decided to transfer the exercise institute to Vienna, which was still one of the capital cities of music. We can guess at the ulterior motive. On the way there, he visits Dresden and

Prague, and in July he marries his young assistant, Mathilde Scherer. Before long there is no word being said about plans for a new institute, but the chronicle of the year that follows could have been the story of an artistic breakthrough.

Berwald is unimaginably productive. He finally completes the first version of an opera, *Estrella di Soria*, presented at a trial performance in the young family's home, where the author Franz Grillparzer is to be found among the guests. He writes four single-movement orchestral pieces in a genre which ten years later would be called a "symphonic poem" and would be cultivated by composers like Liszt, Smetana, César Franck, and Richard Strauss. He finishes the first version of the *Sinfonie sérieuse*.

And he is conducted by, among others, the celebrated Georg Hellmesberger of the Royal Opera.

And he is well received. In the *Wiener Zeitung für Kunst, Literatur, Theater und Mode*, Carl Kunt — who was, according to the great Hanslick, Vienna's most influential writer of the time — writes that he had listened to Berwald's music with genuine pleasure:

"Lively temperament, romantic fullness, boldness of phrasing and harmony speak to us. He plays on his orchestra as on a keyboard, and manipulates form with an improviser's facility."

The journal is dated March 6th, 1842. On March 15th, at four o'clock in the morning, Mr. and Mrs. Berwald set out on their journey to Stockholm. They arrive on April 19th. They haven't hurried, but it's a long way. They are in the far north.

From the vantage point of Stockholm, they must have seemed a cosmopolitan couple. Mathilde had been born in Germany, but was also of French stock. She spoke two languages fluently, but not until she was in Sweden did she have to set about learning Swedish, which she did successfully.

Franz had been away for thirteen years.

A biographical work from the 1840s has an illustrated page with the nine leading Swedish composers. There was a Berwald there too: his cousin Johan Fredrik, the conductor of the Royal Opera House Orchestra. Franz is Swedish in Berlin and Vienna, but German in Stockholm.

On May 27th, 1842, immediately after that unfortunate introductory concert, the Academy of Music had an election meeting, and Franz Berwald was proposed as a member. Nothing came of it. Not until 1864 was he found worthy. A list of all the wine-merchants and manufacturers whom the Academy up to that point found more interesting would certainly merit a little study, from the viewpoint of eternity.

It is at this time that Berwald is writing symphonies which, from the perspective of 1995, can be ranged among the great European concerts around the middle of the century. But who is he writing for? Few people are listening. What they get to hear is crude foreshadowings. The dreamed-of orchestra is still a long way off.

Only his ideas exist, spectrally evoked on manuscript paper. The fact that they have managed to survive in a comprehensible form is — when one considers it more closely — a miracle.

IV.

Gradually, Berwald now begins to accept his double life.

In the summer of 1846, they travel abroad again, first to Paris — "the object of my most ardent desire," Mathilde writes. They arrive there on July 26th.

If Mr. and Mrs. Berwald's life during the next

few years had been depicted in modern journalistic terms, they would have figured as famous people: famous for being famous, to use Boorstin's classic formulation. They have exactly the right sort of contacts, and help, as soon as they need it, from the Swedish minister. (He had been in charge of the Stockholm Opera when Franz was a member of the orchestra, so they have something in common.)

They encounter international celebrities like the librettist and playwright Halévy and the composer Auber, they must have heard Chopin; and they are present at Berlioz's "so-called Requiem" in St. Eustache's church. Mathilde raves about it in her diary.

Mathilde obtains two standing tickets in Auber's own box for the concerts given by the orchestra of the Academy of Music, and Berwald has high hopes of being played himself if the opportunity arises. Auber promises to include a symphony in the general programme for 1848–49, maintains Mathilde, who is a public relations gift — charming, good-humoured, quick to laugh, and ever loyal to her "little Penn," as she calls the forbidding Franz.

Now they can also, week by week, hear what first-class orchestral playing sounds like and how one gets it to sound like that: through rehearsals.

Many years later Franz Berwald relates in an article how the conductor Habeneck, when he had to study Beethoven's Seventh Symphony, was allowed twenty-one rehearsals. We can easily guess what Franz thinks. When his own *Sinfonie sérieuse* was played so wretchedly in Stockholm, there had been time for only a single rehearsal. The difference in levels of music-making between Stockholm and Paris could even be measured in numbers of working hours.

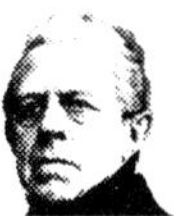

So it goes on. Franz travels further, to Vienna, establishes important new musical contacts, has his music performed, gives concerts in the Austrian provinces, meets with "thunderous applause" in Linz, scores a success in Salzburg, and is elected an honorary fellow of the Mozarteum — and this long before he is admitted to the Academy of Music in Stockholm. "Member of the Mozarteum in Salzburg" is the only musical title he uses from now on. He is proud of that one.

He crops up in interesting contexts. He receives a couple of very fine reviews. With a little re-touching, one could draw up a portrait of a successful career.

What happens is the opposite. Crises roll over Europe. Revolution threatens. Money is not forthcoming. Two music dealers who are close to Berwald go bankrupt. For the first time in his life he begins to despair.

Moreover, life has become yet more complicated. In November, his son Hjalmar is born. There are three of them now. They decide to return to Stockholm, but get stuck in Lübeck.

Catastrophe! The letter sent home to the king in Stockholm on May 3rd, 1849, is a study in wretchedness. Berwald bows and scrapes. He regrets that, despite the king's kindness, he has never "brought in any revenue." He confesses himself in this time of uproar to be "a peace-loving artist who prefers to occupy himself with harmonious combinations rather than with discordant revolutionary yells." Therefore he has fled before the storm with all possible speed! Home!

These were the sentiments a king would be

very pleased to hear in times of upheaval, but Berwald's description of Berwald is new. He is in trouble now, it's obvious.

The years in Europe are over. He didn't think they would end like this. He is fifty-three years old, with a young wife and a newborn son, and he is returning home, as he writes himself, "destitute."

Money arrives from the king. The family takes the boat from Lübeck to Stockholm. A new life begins, and clearly they are also helped to start afresh. This is the period of rich patrons, and what was Berwald's royal patron compared to Wagner's?

In the autumn, Franz Berwald is once again busy composing. On October 27th he completes a string quartet in A-flat; on November 6th, ten days later, a string quartet in E-flat major. They are two masterpieces of austere romantic classicism, exemplifying what maturity signifies in musical creativity.

The string quartet as an ensemble is of its very nature polyphonic: sonorous but polyphonic. The best string quartets give each musician a role in the ensemble, melodic responses which enrich the conversation, and allow each player to feel involved. The string quartet is the greatest triumph of humanism in musical history: the manifestation of human dignity.

If I wish to clarify this reasoning, I am as happy to choose Berwald's quartets as Beethoven's. Obviously I do not need to compare them. My experience of great music is that what is best is what I happen to be listening to at the moment. Presence in time — that it exists now, at this exact moment — is still, in the end, the decisive quality of music. But a movement of a Berwald quartet also has its effect precisely because of its presence. This disciplined music, with its carefully controlled structure, is so light and spontaneous in tone that it might have been born on the instant.

I can whistle to myself the characteristic theme from the Quartet in E-flat major — it happens — but each time I listen to it I am still astonished by the tonal perfection, by the conversation between the instruments, by felicitous interjections from the viola here, the cello there. Berwald's strictly disciplined music is written as if for fun.

Look at his face!

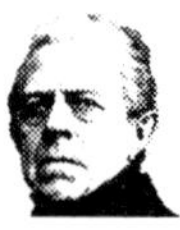

Why the string quartet? We know that one of Berwald's acquaintances was Ludvig Petré, a rather younger man in his thirties. Music must have brought them together. Petré was a businessman, and at the time was doing well. He owned a complete set of stringed instruments, including a Stradivarius. That would have been enough motivation for Berwald to pursue the friendship. Now he is enclosed within a new social format, and life is possible again.

Swedish musical life at that time was not highly organized, and the Royal Opera Orchestra was the only largish orchestra in the land. On the other hand, there were a number of musical coteries, where all kinds of small-scale music were cultivated. Berwald came across a string quartet. So he wrote for string quartet, and out of what he wrote there bespeaks something to which I can give no other name but happiness.

A new epoch in Berwald's life begins, and surprising changes follow. Ludvig Petré owns Sandö glassworks in Norrland. In 1850, Berwald becomes managing director there. The era of commercial enterprise in Swedish history has begun. He is successful at his work and stays there for eight years, adapting to a new yearly rhythm: winter in Stockholm, the summer half of the year up north.

Berwald becomes a well-to-do member of the Stockholm middle classes. He makes pungent contributions to the cultural debate; takes on gifted music students who, in a few cases, grow to international calibre; becomes a source of support for younger colleagues; and even, finally, becomes a teacher at the Academy of Music, composing in his spare time, not least chamber music. In time he gains prestige, but not more than his rivals in the lists can manage to live with. He is a cultivated and undoubtedly also a chastened man who has put all thoughts of a musical career out of his mind. Perhaps.

Yet he keeps trying to get the Stockholm Opera to put on *Estrella di Soria,* succeeds finally in 1862, then writes yet another opera, *The Queen of Golconda.* Old love is not soon forgotten, they say, but who is to say that it must have a happy ending? Nevertheless, the fact remains that the overture to *Estrella di Soria* is a sparkling orchestral piece to grace a concert programme.

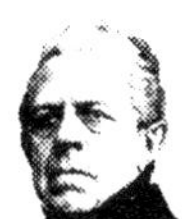

What strikes an onlooker in the year 1995 is that practically all of Berwald's artistically substantial music remained private. The symphonies were written for the public, but were never played in Berwald's lifetime — if we turn a mercifully blind eye to the wretched performance of *Sinfonie sérieuse* in 1843. The late string quartets were never printed and seem never to have been played in public. The chamber-music pieces for strings and piano are characterized by an exclusivity which makes the best of them into everlasting companions, but never to the degree that they throw themselves on the listener's neck.

For myself, I keep coming back to the Piano Trio in D minor of 1851. It is like a classical landscape, in creative repose, divided between light and shadow. I find it impossible not to believe that when Berwald was in Vienna he heard Schumann's 1847 piano trio in the same key. To my ears, Berwald's trio is like an act of homage. One master pays homage to another master with a masterpiece, but his home is his castle.

At the same time, there is an interesting difference: in the piano texture. The pianist Robert Schumann wrote the piano part for the hand. Berwald wrote for the ear, in a way which was "un-pianistic," as it's usually called, and very difficult. Yet as piano technique developed, that difference came more and more to be transformed into a difference in expressiveness. Modern instrumentalists are a hardened breed. They regard difficulties as a challenge. In this way, difficulties are reflected in performance as a projection of work, like compressed time.

To that extent musicians have caught up with Berwald. Sometimes the thought occurs that only now, for the first time, is it possible to hear his music as it sounded in his imagination: heavy and weightless, free of the inertia of the matter. I am strengthened in this conviction by gramophone recordings from different periods. The record label Caprice has issued two very interesting and instructive CDs of historic material, one with symphonic music by Berwald interpreted by two different conductors (*Berwald x 2*); the other with older recordings of Swedish string-quartet ensembles, who naturally also play Berwald.

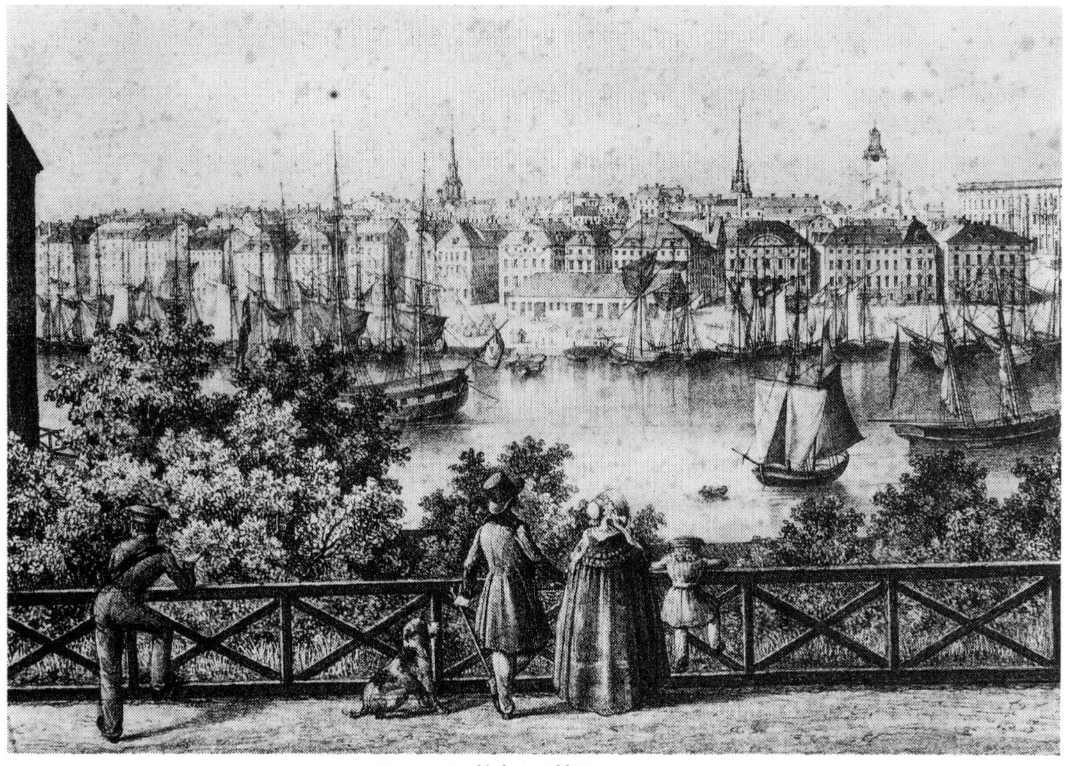

View of Stockholm's Old Town, 1840s.

This gives a historical perspective which has not existed before our own time.

The essential question is, self-evidently, what have we gained and lost by our new perfectionism: presumably we have gained in clarity but lost in sensibility. In Berwald's case, though, there is another aspect to consider, which I personally think is more important. Clarity exposes Berwald and creates a new sonority. I like to think that what I hear in the best modern recordings approaches what Berwald heard inwardly when he wrote notes down on paper. In the older recordings, on the other hand, I hear the romantic surge but I miss the part-writing and illumination that let me gaze deep down into the wells of thought.

And that is why I have such high hopes for this two-hundredth anniversary celebration. One hundred and fifty years was too short a time, I see that now. The orchestras had not progressed sufficiently far in control and coordination. After all, the development of orchestral technique in the electronic age, and conducting technique, and rehearsal technique has changed our sense of tone and given us a new perception of the resources of human hearing.

This is not indisputably to our advantage, not for all music. There is an opposition between suggestion and clarity, and if the romantic surge is lost, the dreams and longing are deprived of broad areas of wavelength. But Berwald perhaps finds his contemporaries for the first time among those of us who are alive now.

Sometimes, when I hear a work like *Sinfonie singulière,* I can get it into my head that it still cannot be played as it was conceived. Perhaps in time the first theme of the finale can be played in such a way that no one can be mistaken as to how the lines of force run; so that everyone hears the syncopes. We who are alive now have the possibility of maintaining that relationship to music. What we want to get to know we will play again.

I should perhaps qualify what I have said: Berwald might not encounter his contemporaries until tomorrow. He will encounter them first when we have generally accepted that some music appeals to us most only when we need it, and need it alone. In our time, musical experiences that come close to the experience of lyric poetry are made possible, even when one has been listening to large orchestras or operatic ensembles. Here we are like the princes of old. Our resources are infinite, our freedom of movement total.

Nor is it of any importance for a composer like Berwald if it becomes obvious that exclusivity is his trademark. It may well be that all those promising flops with which his path through life were strewn came about because, with that very existential quality, he addressed himself to the few.

But what does it matter in these days when one can access a database wherever there happens to be a telephone line or a satellite connection, and ask for Berwald, Franz, String Quartet in E-flat major to be played immediately, in a recording he would have approved of himself? In Ulan Bator. In St. Louis, Missouri. At Drottninggatan in Stockholm, where he lived. What does exclusivity mean then? Why should a Berwald care?

As for inaccessibility, it should not be exaggerated. One of our century's great conductors, Fritz Busch, who had close and longstanding Swedish contacts, made a telling remark about Berwald: "He is fresh and blue like the Swedish sky in May."

May, our loveliest month.

Translated from the Swedish by Harry D. Watson

ALF THOOR, born in 1923, is a longtime collaborator in Swedish press, radio, and TV, in culture and politics, for periods as a music critic. In 1977–88 he served as editorial page editor of the large daily Expressen. HARRY D. WATSON is editor of the *Dictionary of the Older Scottish Tongue,* University of Edinburgh. In this issue, he has also translated Magnus Florin's "The Garden."

Letter to the Editors

Dear Editors,

I've read the entire issue of Artes no. 2, stimulated by much of what's here: The Nobel Lecture, Per Wästberg's piece on Jules Verne, Leif Zern on Ingmar Bergman (especially intriguing — the mirror symbolism on p. 57), and Professor Perloff's insightful reading on Roland Barthes/Christian Boltanski.

Ironically, it is her inability to "read" figure 8 (# 86) completely that led to my own professional approach to the photo's closure.

What is actually the reality — if one takes the time to dissect and "read" the photo — is that there are two seesaws side by side, supported by a metal bar; but, because of the lack of depth-of-field combined with the meshing of silhouettes, it appears they're on top of one another: the standing, somewhat crouched, figure is facing the child whose legs are dangling, seemingly suspended in midair. However, that child's body-silhouette is completely absorbed by the standing figure in the far right of the frame.

But, in looking more closely, we see that there are actually three seesaws, evidenced by the three horizontal, tightly knit shadows stretching thinly across the ground in the bottom of the frame. The one nearest the camera and the one next to it are at corresponding angles to each other, while the third (the one with crouched figure) is more or less at an opposite angle. While the standing figure to the far right actually holds down the seesaw in balance, the partner's slight kneebend gives the seesaw its suspended tension. Fascinating. I'm surprised this wasn't looked at more closely.

Gerard Malanga

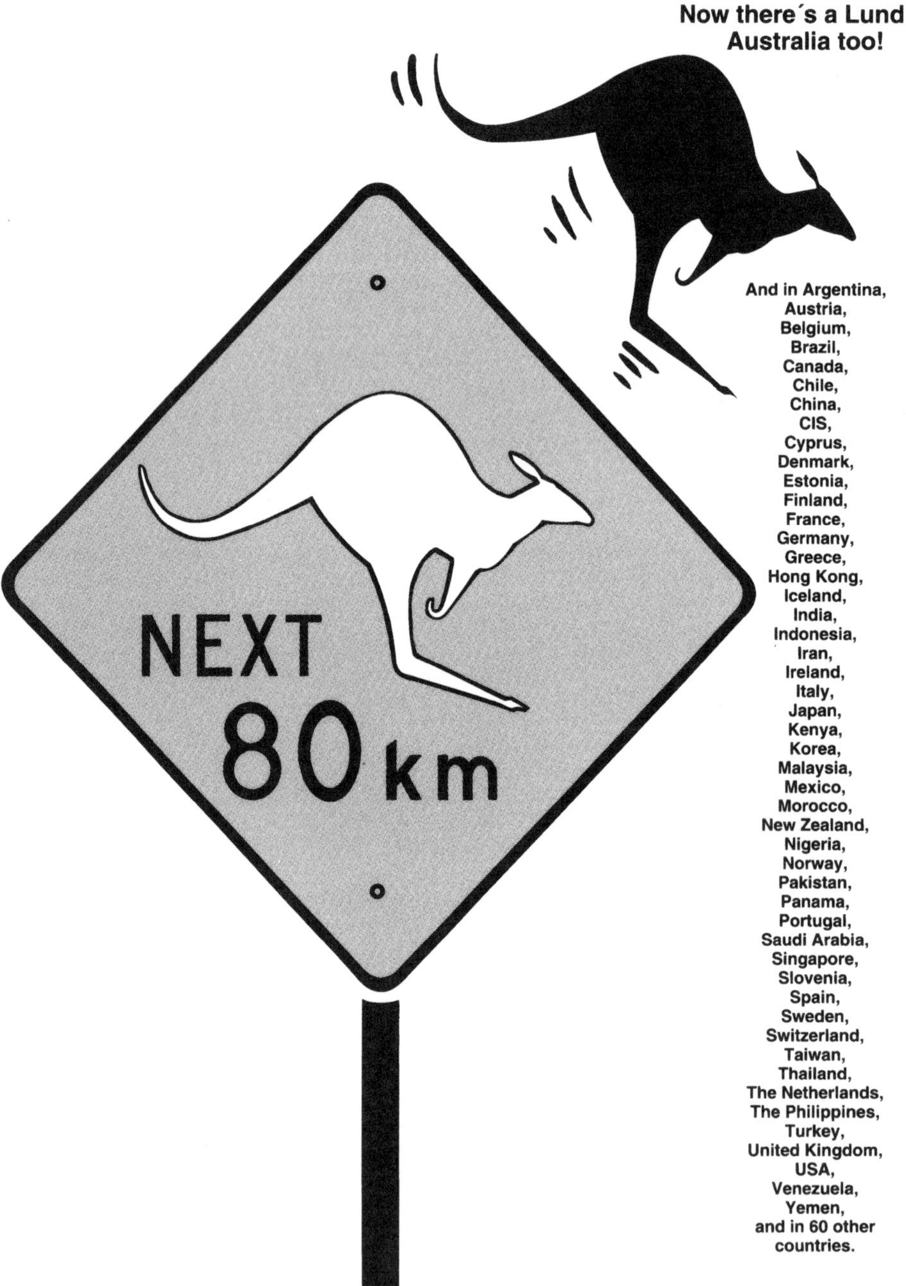

Tetra Pak today extends to the four corners of the world. All of Tetra Pak´s customers and personnel, in whatever country, know that it began in Lund.

And for us that´s very important. Our success depends on a good basic concept, which has proved suitable for all climates and for all cultures – the concept of making the distribution of essential products like milk, water and juices as simple as possible.

We know that ideas, human ideas, are the key to success.

That´s why ideas, know-how and creativity have always come top of our list.

Tetra Pak

Linde & Co

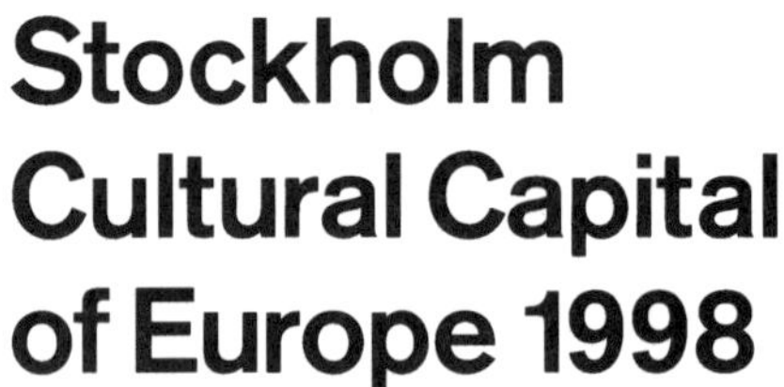

Stockholm Cultural Capital of Europe 1998

Global Meeting Place
Freedom of Speech
Sound and Silence
The City as Stage
Stockholism
Spaces of the Past
Roots and Rites
Generation K
Folk Creativities
Aurora Borealis
Waterways
Light and Darkness
Designs for Living
Green Spaces
In Leonardo's Footsteps

In 1998 Stockholm is the Cultural Capital of Europe.

The city of Stockholm has formed an organization working to present a really extraordinary set of events lasting throughout 1998.

The suggestions of a large number of people have inspired the efforts to formulate fifteen "anchor themes" (left) for 1998.

In addition, children's culture will play a comprehensive role as an overall theme and the culture of Sweden as a whole will occupy the spotlight.

For further information:

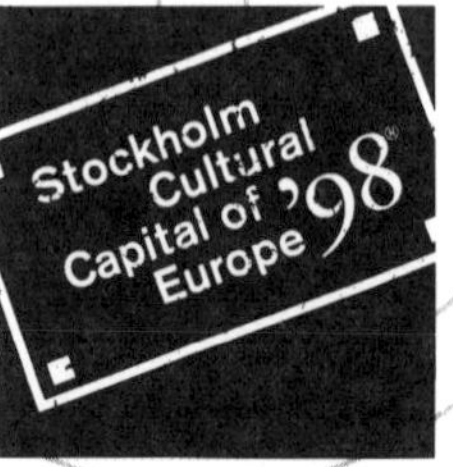

STOCKHOLM – CULTURAL CAPITAL OF EUROPE 1998
Street address: Sergels Torg 12, 4tr.
Mailing address: Box 7313, 103 90 Stockholm.
Telephone: +46 08-402 24 40.
Telefax: +46 08-24 99 16.
E-mail: info@kultur98.stockholm.se
Internet: www.kultur98.stockholm.se